WHO IS IN THE ROOM?

With this book, Brooke O'Harra takes up directing as an artistic practice in and of itself. Speaking beyond and against craft, O'Harra drives the art of directing forward.

O'Harra investigates a series of important questions: How do we wrest our work from institutional imperatives of public building and culture building? How can an artist-driven discourse lead us toward the urgencies of artists and their publics in this moment? How do we "make" plays? How do we activate the relationships of making, whether between artists in the rehearsal room or between the production and the audience? Brooke addresses all aspects of the directorial process: reckoning with the script through dramaturgy, working within the rehearsal room, collaborating with other artists, as well as staging and production.

This exploration will be of great interest to students and scholars in performance studies with a particular interest in directing.

Brooke O'Harra teaches acting and directing, queer performance practices, and experimental playwriting at the University of Pennsylvania, USA.

Routledge Advances in Theatre & Performance Studies

This series is our home for cutting-edge, upper-level scholarly studies and edited collections. Considering theatre and performance alongside topics such as religion, politics, gender, race, ecology, and the avant-garde, titles are characterized by dynamic interventions into established subjects and innovative studies on emerging topics.

Messy Connections
Creating Atmospheres of Addiction Recovery Through Creative Performance Practice
Cathy Sloan

To Repair the World
Zelda Fichandler and the Transformation of American Theater
Mary B. Robinson

LO:TECH:POP:CULT
Screendance Remixed
Priscilla Guy, Alanna Thain

The Shakespeare North Playhouse
Replica Theatres and their Uses
Timothy F Keenan

The Art of Entertainment
Popular Performance in Modern British Art, 1880 to 1940
Jason Price

The Routledge Companion to Performance-Related Concepts in Non-European Languages
Erika Fischer-Lichte, Torsten Jost, Astrid Schenka

The Legacy of Stylistic Theatre in the Creation of a Modern Sinhala Drama in Sri Lanka
Lakshmi D Bulathsinghala

Passion and Elegance
How Flamenco and Classical Ballet Met at the Ballets Russes
Barbara Marangon

The Canon in Contemporary Theatre
Plays by Shakespeare, Ibsen, and Brecht in Contemporary Directors' Theatre
Lars Harald Maagerø

Who Is In the Room?
Queer Strategies for Redefining the Role of the Theater Director
Brooke O'Harra

For more information about this series, please visit: www.routledge.com/Routledge-Advances-in-Theatre--Performance-Studies/book-series/RATPS

WHO IS IN THE ROOM?

Queer Strategies for Redefining the Role of the Theater Director

Brooke O'Harra

Routledge
Taylor & Francis Group

LONDON AND NEW YORK

Cover image: photo by Julieta Cervantes

First published 2025
by Routledge
4 Park Square, Milton Park, Abingdon, Oxon OX14 4RN

and by Routledge
605 Third Avenue, New York, NY 10158

Routledge is an imprint of the Taylor & Francis Group, an informa business

British Library Cataloguing-in-Publication Data
A catalogue record for this book is available from the British Library

Library of Congress Cataloging-in-Publication Data
Names: O'Harra, Brooke, 1973– author.
Title: Who is in the room?: queer strategies for redefining the role of the theater director / Brooke O'Harra.
Description: London; New York: Routledge, 2024. |
Series: Routledge series in equity, diversity, and inclusion in theatre and performance |
Includes bibliographical references and index. |
Identifiers: LCCN 2024004464 (print) | LCCN 2024004465 (ebook) |
ISBN 9781032182032 (hbk) | ISBN 9781032181974 (pbk) | ISBN 9781003253402 (ebk)
Subjects: LCSH: Theater—Production and direction. | Gay theater. | LCGFT: Essays.
Classification: LCC PN2053 O425 2024 (print) | LCC PN2053 (ebook) |
DDC 792.02/33—dc23/eng/20240617
LC record available at https://lccn.loc.gov/2024004464
LC ebook record available at https://lccn.loc.gov/2024004465

ISBN: 9781032182032 (hbk)
ISBN: 9781032181974 (pbk)
ISBN: 9781003253402 (ebk)

DOI: 10.4324/9781003253402

Typeset in Sabon
by codeMantra

CONTENTS

Acknowledgments   *vi*
Preface   *viii*

Essay One. I'm Bleeding All Over the Place: Queer Auteur Director   1

Card Catalog   17

Essay Two. Brings Us Together and Keeps Us Apart   23

Essay Three. Deep Listening, or I Can't Tell You How To Do That Play   37

Essay Four. Who Is Joan Littlewood? Or The Impossibility of the Auteur   48

Essay Five. Actors! Let Them Be Astonishing   60

Essay Six. The Education of the Director (In Three Parts)   72

Your UNTEXTBOOK   90

Index   *109*

ACKNOWLEDGMENTS

I would not have written this book or become a queer auteur director without the work I did running the theater company, Theater of a Two-headed Calf, for 15 years. And I would never have done that if it weren't for the persistence and unabated optimism of my brilliant co-founder, composer Brendan Connelly. Thank you so much, Brendan.

It was Ellen Stewart, Nicky Paraiso, and the folks at La Mama Experimental Theater Club who gave me my first theatrical home and showed me the truth of the room, of the community, of care, and of saying "Yes!" My gratitude to them runs deep.

I learned so much from the Dyke Division (of Two-headed Calf) and the collaborators with whom I dreamed up the world of Sappho, MA for the live lesbian serial drama *Room for Cream*: Jess Barbagallo, Laryssa Husiak, Laura Berlin-Stinger, and eventually Barbara Lanciers and Sasha Yanow. Each of you is such a gift to me. *Room for Cream* was foundationally transformative for me as a person, a director, and a performance maker; and this transformation happened because of and through my interactions with the amazing casts, actors and non-actors alike, who made up our weekly ensembles as well as, significantly, the audiences who filled the seats of the La Mama Club theater to share in the world with us.

Collaborators! The many incredible actors with whom I have worked showed me how to be in the room for them and how to work with them, as did so many designers, playwrights, and musicians. You know who you are. Thank you especially to those artists who worked with me for a decade or more: Tina Shepard, Heidi Schreck, Becca Blackwell, Mike Mikos, Justin Townsend, Peter Ksander, Russell Greenberg, and Laura Barger.

Rosemary Quinn and Roger Babb first asked me to teach theater, and I thank them for making me a teacher. And thanks to all of my students, past, present, and future, who made and make me a good teacher.

Heather Love read this book numerous times during this process. I thank her for her many very good notes and unrelenting encouragement. The Wednesday writing pod made up of Matthew Battles, Rob Handel, and Kio Stark and formed under the leadership of Karinne Keithley Syers engaged the book as it grew from lists and rants to essays. Thank you for your whimsy and for indulging me at every stage. Ross Gay, Kristen

Kosmas, Jess Barbagallo, Bethany Schneider, Amitav Ghosh, Bryna Turner, Agnes Borinsky, and Dana Bishop-Root each read some or all of the manuscript when I was in need of support and feedback.

I started this book through the Bassini Apprenticeship at the University of Pennsylvania because my friend and colleague Julia Bloch (director of Creative Writing) asked me if I was writing a book and I said, "I could." It was the student apprentices Claris Park and Seung Hyun Chung who helped me launch into this research and helped me steer toward what I could offer to a larger public. I am so grateful to you three for creating a pathway for this project to begin.

I would like to thank my series editor Bren Foley who invited me to write the book for Routledge and, in doing so, willed me to finish it. I extend that gratitude to my editor Laura Hussey and to Swatti Hindwan. Thank you for making this book with me.

I couldn't have done this without the support of my family. My mother Kris, a teacher and an author of textbooks and memoir, combed through my writing and gave expert advice on grammar and style. My partner Sharon Hayes engaged this project at every step of the process - making time to read drafts, work through ideas and help me find my way towards my voice. Her support and attention has been extraordinary and is always given with such grace, love, and patience. And I thank my daughter Alice who loves to act and who at the age of twelve already has a deep commitment to equity and community. You, my family, make me want to live with passion and care.

PREFACE

Who Is in the Room?

If this were a rehearsal and we were gathered to work together, I would begin with a question. I always begin with a question. So, here in this book, I begin:

"Who is in the room?"

I'd like to think one answer would be **me** and **you**. Here we are together. Hi.

Maybe that makes you wonder, "What kind of room is this?" – this book. This room that we are talking about is a room in which we try to conceive of the theater as a place of expansive possibility for each of us.

The question "Who is in the (rehearsal) room?" teases at other questions: "Who has the privilege to be in the room?" "Who do you want in the room?" or "What do you want to happen in that room?" Those lead us to the question, "Why has that wanting felt like such an impossible ask for queer people, people of color, and even for women?" For so many of us, the stakes of gathering together have always been high. Underlying these questions is the proposition that, as theater and performance makers, we are tasked with assessing the value of shared time and space and recognizing our responsibility, as artists and as spectators, to make meaning together.

In this book, I want to reimagine the terms of the director's work, empowering directors to think like auteurs and queer their work. I will address all aspects of the directorial process: collaborating with other artists, working within the rehearsal room, reckoning with the script through dramaturgy, as well as staging and production. This, however, is not a "how-to" book nor is it a series of personal anecdotes (although I do use anecdotes). Instead, by engaging the critical knowledge a director will need throughout the process of putting on a play, I encourage you to use knowledge about directing as a jumping-off point to explore/discover the director as a practitioner and, as in my case, a queer auteur director.

I have adopted the essay form. I believe the essay best supports my core arguments that the director is a critical thinker who uses an understanding of theatrical form to open up both the possibilities of the text and the possibilities of rigorous collaboration. The essay is both critical and conversational, moving between observation and theoretical critique. As with my stage work, I intend that these essays be a little bit playful, a little bit confrontational, while advocating for nothing less than radical change to the work of culture making.

Radical Change Now

The act of coming together to make theater, whether that be to make the work (in the rehearsal room) or to share work (in the theater), has always been an unstable proposition – often built on loose assumptions of shared expectations, potential affinities, and unspoken political desire.

In mid-March 2020, we all began working (or not working) in isolation from our colleagues and collaborators, following recommendations for precautions necessitated by the COVID-19 global pandemic. Suddenly the power and necessity of being in a room together came into sharp focus. The loss of our ability to gather, and thus create and produce live theater and performance, created a vacuum and reminded us of our field's utter dependence on gathering as bodies in real time and in shared space.

The partial lockdown was followed by the very public murder of George Floyd on May 25, 2020, igniting another wave of protests over the deep violence of systemic racism in the US with demands for justice and change. These calls for change spread beyond the streets and into institutions, including most arts institutions. These demands are not new; the need for radical change is not new. But what feels different is the possibility that the ground was shaken enough that foundations can be reimagined.

This book of essays is meant to address the possibilities of making necessary changes in the theater through the work of the director, and more specifically using the role of queer auteur director as a position from which we can consider these urgencies. Changing the theater may not change the world, but we can carve out spaces that allow for new voices to create the terms of coming together.

While writing this, I have been working toward questions of refusing the current power structures of institutions and funders – asking instead that we nurture and allow for aesthetics, desire, and personal politics while bringing a play to an audience. In other words, I have imagined the influences and voices that determine who is in the room.

We Gather Here

Identity is intersectional. And I want to be clear that my use of queer holds the expansive identities of queer folx: native, two-spirited, transgender, genderqueer, Black, brown, Asian, and South Pacific Islanders. I acknowledge my debt to the black women and trans-women who played a critical role in gay liberation. In this book, I discuss claiming spaces and narratives. These discussions are intended in allyship with the important collective work happening to decolonize the fields of theater and performance.

The land I make work on is stolen land. This is a book of essays that will return regularly to the question of who is in the room: meaning who feels welcome, who is heard, who determines the terms, who gets support, and who gets to claim space. But what does it mean to claim space on land that was so violently and brutally taken?

It means that we work toward repair by allowing the room to be a space of experimentation and worldmaking that allows experts exist in all communities – that there are audiences waiting to have work made for them. These are the conditions in which we make work. These are the conditions of the room in which we gather.

Essay One

I'M BLEEDING ALL OVER THE PLACE

Queer Auteur Director

"You are very creative." A total stranger said this to me on a beach on the shore of Lake Superior. She was walking her dog, and I was just standing there, distracted and lost in thought. It was around 20 degrees outside and, though this was warm for northern Minnesota in January, it wasn't the kind of weather you linger in, particularly not on the breezy shoreline. But the scenery was stunning, and there was an otherworldly sound coming off the lake caused by massive sheets of ice bumping up against one another. It would have been a waste of a day, or a trip – or a life, even – to have not taken a moment to be there. And there I was. The first thing the woman said to me was actually, "You must be sad." I wasn't sad. I explained that I was just thinking. I was thinking about a project I had been working on. I was chasing my thoughts, and I was braiding them with the moment, the beauty. I told her I was a director, and I had a theater company in New York, and I was writing a grant. She asked if I had written a lot of plays. I explained that I was a director, not a playwright. She looked baffled. I tried to explain what a director does. She listened. She smiled. Then she said "you are very creative" and continued walking her dog down the beach. And I was thinking that is such a ridiculous thing to say. How could she even know whether or not I was *creative*? This woman, out with her dog in below-freezing temperatures who has no idea what a director does, determined that I am creative. Ha!

I often find that people don't know what a director does, and they can't fully conceive of the role of a director as a *creative* one. It would take me more than my two hands to count the number of times I have been introduced (sometimes by people who know my work well!) as a *playwright*. I think this happens because people understand quite well that I make things and that I have a practice, but they cannot quite settle on a title for what I do. They recognize that I have a kind of authorship and voice in my projects, and this leaves them grasping for a term to express what that is. The word *director* doesn't seem quite right, and maybe *playwright* gets them a little closer to how they name authorship.

I direct plays and frequently work with playwrights. Typically, I do not devise work or build my projects from improvisation. I am very much a director. For me, directing is something akin to authoring; it involves having a point of view and building a project

DOI: 10.4324/9781003253402-1

through a practice. If you need a better way to describe me and my practice, it could be to call me a queer auteur director. That feels correct. You might, while introducing me, say, "This is my friend Brooke. She is a queer auteur director." Aside: *I have never been introduced that way. . . as of yet.*

Queer + Auteur

Why queer?

To be a *queer* artist requires a constant stretch and renegotiation of language, positionality, and possibilities of desire. To be a *queer* auteur director is to alter and open one's gaze inside a field of desires and impulses that necessarily skew away from the normative onslaught dictated by dominant (theater) culture. These norms encompass how we perform desire, how we represent beauty, but even how we order reason and orient our movements. As we insist on queer slang, we go gayly forward not straight ahead. My definition of queer is necessarily broad and takes cues from Ariel Goldberg's book of essays *The Estrangement Principle*. Goldberg digs deep into definitions of the "queer artist" and arrives at this argument:

> 'Queer' in relation to art, constantly reinvents itself. Loosely aligned with a range of identity positions counter to mass culture, 'queer' resembles an umbrella one buys that falls apart shortly after a rainstorm. Anything can be interpreted and argued for as 'queer.'[1]

Countering the frequent complaint against the word queer that with its self-understanding anything can be "it," Goldberg suggests that allusiveness and slipperiness are the very things that make queer *queer*. They call this "the pact of the word queer, to resist the task of definition altogether."[2]

For me being queer does not only hold my lesbian identity, but it is also a kind of stand-in or shorthand for my politics and my investments in justice. My queerness carries a commitment to a whole range of things that matter to me and my community. It's why I am a block leader in my West Philadelphia neighborhood and why I volunteer with mutual aid programs. My queerness keeps me out in my front yard cultivating an all-season flower garden so people will stop as they walk by and take a picture or smell the lilacs. My queer family organized a Sunday afternoon dance party every week on our street during the Covid lockdown.

Certainly, it was because I am queer that I became a director. Yet I was a director before I ever acknowledged that I was queer. It was through my choice to be a theater director that I could find my way to my queerness. Being a director in the theater created the space for me to come out as both a lesbian and a political being.

Why auteur?

The title auteur director, like queer, is often othered or used, by theater producers, to describe someone outside the norm. This othering is produced by/as fear: fear that the auteur theater director might be contrarian that they'll make their own rules, question the norms; that they'll undermine the structures that institutions rely on by creating their own systems. Yes, this is true, auteur directors often do.

The term **auteur** circulates more frequently in cinema as a description for film directors who use a singular style, vision, or approach to their filmmaking. Emerging in the 1950s out of film criticism and the practices and investments of directors of the French New Wave, auteurs develop and employ techniques that allow for a viewing experience that pushes beyond the film's script; they have been described as using the camera as a pen and making radical cinematic choices to illicit deeper connections to their subjects. Chantal Akerman, Claire Denis, and Agnès Varda, for example, are auteurs who radically transformed how women's lives are portrayed on film – through the tactical and conceptual inhabitation of their own gaze as makers. The use of **gaze** here suggests both an intimate and personal way of seeing and reading the world as well as a methodological investment in how their way of seeing translates to new forms of seeing for an audience.

Although this terminology is less frequently used in the theater, there are **theater auteurs or auteur theater directors**. To be an auteur theater director does not necessitate rebellion, but is to fundamentally accept that making happens in and of the present moment. For the auteur theater director, even the most classical of scripts must be "remade" in the present moment – not interpreted for the present, but found and (co) authored anew. You need more than the script or the playwright to do that.

What I'd like you to consider is that, for me, there is no tension between queer and auteur because a queer auteur theater director might be more homemade or grassroots or ground-up in their practice. In other words, queer auteur should not invoke the "dude who wears sunglasses inside" (Fellini! 8½!) or "the genius who has a signature style." On the contrary, the queer auteur may even be obscure or invisible; their efforts may instead support the strengths of everyone in the room, drawing attention to the performers or the writer with whom they are working. And that is also okay. As you grasp for a word to describe what you do, consider whether you, too, are a queer auteur director.

I'm Bleeding All Over the Place: Studies in directing, or nine encounters between you and me

This book of essays is the final "event" of a multi-year performance project that served as active research on the subject of directing. *I'm Bleeding All Over the Place: Studies in directing or nine encounters between me and you,* a series of performance events that I called "studies in directing," is a project that allowed me to work, in real time in front of audiences, to investigate liveness, conflict, and intimacy in the theater. This project made it possible to interrogate the very issues that I address in this book in front of/with a live audience. This is the ninth encounter between me and you. For the purpose of this encounter, the me *is* me and the you *is* you.

With the project *I'm Bleeding All Over the Place,* I allowed myself to invite chaos and destabilization into a process that I normally control, as director. The title of the project grew out of a confluence of events and desires; but, in part, *bleeding all over the place* marks a desire to *spill out,* to release or lose control, to blur into the place of another, allowing the inside of my work to be visible on the outside.

Over the course of several years, I directed eight events which included seven single-event performances as well as a production that had a longer theatrical run under the general heading *I'm Bleeding All Over the Place;* but each had a separate subtitle:

Are We in Conflict?	New Museum 2014
Show Me	New Museum 2014
It's Personal	New Museum 2014
A Living History Tour	La Mama ETC 2016 – Three-week run
So?	Catch Series at Philadelphia Fringe 2017
In Terms of Performance	Bam Café 2018
Post No Bills	Common Field, Philadelphia 2019
Captive(ated) Audience	Yarn/Wire Gala Ten Ri Institute 2019

The first three performances investigated the audience as author – addressing how the audience projects desire, politics, conflict, and violence onto subjects on stage and into tiny interactions in daily life. The fourth part of the project, *A Living History Tour,* engaged the intimacy of the public realm and more specifically the director's intimate relationship with her audience. This event was followed by two performances that allowed the audience to speak, albeit *en masse*, in the room. The last event was a kind of playful portrait of the trauma I experienced while learning too much about my relationship to my audience. In total, there have been eight "encounters." This book is the ninth and final encounter. It is a direct invitation to you to join me in these studies.

Becoming a Queer Auteur Director

I didn't always identify as a queer auteur director – or even a queer director – or even a director. I was an athlete growing up, and I went to college to study Mechanical Engineering. But in high school, I fell in love with Japanese Cinema and began to study the Japanese language. It was my interest in Japanese cinema that led me to acting classes in college, and it was my acting teacher (an adjunct who had been part of an experimental theater company from the age of 17) and my Japanese language teacher (who loved Japanese theater) who encouraged me to move to Japan to study the language and the theater. My life in the theater started in Tokyo, Japan – first as audience and then as a practitioner. While living and working in Japan, I studied Japanese theater and Aikido. When I wasn't working and training, I saw a great deal of live theater in Tokyo: both traditional Japanese Theater (Kabuki, Noh, Bunraku, Butoh) and touring shows by auteur theater directors and their companies (Ariane Mnouchkine's Théâtre du Soleil, Robert Wilson, Anne Bogart's Siti Company, Simon McBurney's Théâtre de Complicité, Robert LePage's Ex Machina, Elizabeth LeCompt's The Wooster Group). I also discovered that the library in my neighborhood had a large selection of books by theater practitioners in the English-language section. This theater selection was outsized compared to the other English language offerings. I imagine this is because these books did not otherwise exist in translation in the library and that someone at the library or in the community was very interested in directing. I devoured those books, taking copious notes. I read Stanislavsky, Brecht, Brook, Grotowksi, Artaud, etc. As I read their books, I began to long so deeply to be in conversation with these directors. I wanted to do the things they described in their books. So, in the early mornings at my gym, I performed a regimen of exercises described in Grotowski's *Towards a Poor Theater*. Often, I would do this in the aerobics class-room that I shared with Japanese "salarymen" who were practicing their golf swings. We trained together, in a sense. I was unbashful about introducing myself to and befriending young artists actively working in the Japanese theater scene and was subsequently invited to be in several shows with a young Butoh Company in Tokyo because they needed a na-tive English speaker in their show. Eventually, I grew frustrated by working in my own body. I wanted to continue my study by directing actors. I wanted a company to explore the ideas I was absorbing. So, I started a theater company called Mischievium. The com-pany was made up of five foreigners (from Canada, the US, France, and Hong Kong) and five Japanese nationals. We trained and rehearsed in my apartment or a park near my place and created original movement-based plays that we performed in Japanese in Ueno Park, Tokyo. A young Japanese playwriting student wrote original scripts for us. He was fixated on making work that addressed Japan's anti-immigration policies. An Irish com-poser created scores that we made dances for (including one where we danced with our eyes). The plays were only 10 minutes in length because that was about as long as we had before the park police shooed us away; performance in the park was illegal. We put out a collection box that had a sign that said "For Return to Our Home Countries" – the play-wright insisted on that. We collected about $200 for every 10-minute show because, in a city as densely populated as Tokyo, it took 60 seconds to draw an audience of 50 people. We used this money to buy bento lunches for the folks experiencing homelessness who spent their days in the park. When I moved to Japan, this was not my plan – because I had no plan. I was just kind of following my desires and interests, and I just kept saying yes to my own ideas and kept building relationships with folks who shared those interests.

I eventually did "return to my home country" to attend graduate school for direct-ing in New Orleans. Then I moved to New York and, in that same spirit of willing my desires into existence and finding folks to join in, I started The Theater of a Two-headed Calf with composer Brendan Connelly. Aside from Brendan and me, the company was a loose affiliation of theater artists – actors and designers. Our core design team eventu-ally became Justin Townsend and Peter Ksander. Actors worked with the company on a show-by-show basis. But there were regulars like Laryssa Husiak, Heidi Schreck, David Brooks, Mike Mikos, Jess Barbagallo, and Becca Blackwell. We always performed with live musicians, several of whom (Ian Antonio, Laura Barger, and Russell Greenberg) eventually formed the new music ensemble Yarn/Wire. Two-Headed Calf developed and performed 11 shows between 2001 and 2014; all were directed by me.

It wasn't until our seventh show, *Drum of the Waves of Horikawa,* that I started to yearn to be seen by my queer peers. *Drum of the Waves of Horikawa* was a Kabuki drama scored and choreographed for punk rock sound, style, and movement. Because the entire performance drew on the formal relationships between musician and actor, with the actors and musicians working in response to one another, the performance took two and a half years of regular rehearsals, residencies, and workshops to build. As we devel-oped the show, we broke it into sections eventually making it an episodic show, meaning we performed it as five episodes over a two-and-a-half-hour evening. Every detail of the performance was scored and choreographed. Working in this lengthy time frame made it possible to consider and reconsider all of our choices. This kind of attention to detail was necessary because we were attempting to transliterate actor training models from the traditional form, Kabuki, where performers learned their roles through direct imitation of the song and movement of the master of their troupe. We drew from narratives about the origins of Kabuki, specifically the Kabuki dance of Izumo of Okuni who created Kabuki by mimicking the style, dress, and flamboyant behavior of Kabuki-mono. Kabuki-mono was a term used to describe gangs of anti-conformist deviants (often made up of shogun-less samurai) who defied social rules and conventions and protested the established order by donning shocking hairdos, strange facial hair, and women's clothing. Just as Izumo of Okuni copied the style, gesture, and movement of the Kabuki-mono, we copied with precision the arbitrary and wild scores and vocal patterns of hardcore and punk rock performances from the 1980s and 1990s bands and performers like Darby Crash and The Germs, Iggy Pop, Fugazi, Nina Hagen, the Slits, and so on.

In this process, something else started to inform our choices: queerness. Though we hadn't set out to make a specifically queer show, it became legibly queer and cultivated a queer following. I had chosen that particular Kabuki text because the plot is arguably feminist. But while casting clever women and disempowered lusty men, I gravitated to filling these roles with the queer performers Laryssa Husiak, Laura Berlin-Stinger, and Jess Barbagallo. These actors' very embodiment complicated the gender roles. In fact, every casting choice we made undermined typical stereotypes of the male hero, the villain, the lowly maid, and the victimized female. This project was more queer than any I had previously made. And somehow word got out that something delightfully homo was happening downtown, and the queer folks showed up. I was already feeling the joy of having so many lesbians in the room with me, but once the audience started to reflect us there was no turning back for me (Figure 1.1).

FIGURE 1.1   Heidi Schreck as Otane and Jess Barbagallo as Ee'sSoGay YouGayMan in *Drum of the Waves of Horikawa* at Here Arts Center, NYC 2007.

Could I Have Some *Room for Cream*, Please?

The total response to *Drum* was a huge surprise for me because I knew we were addressing a public, but I had no idea how to bring them in. The work of making theater is not just in the making of it. It also demands that you invite the audience into the room with you. I had struggled with the task of promoting *Drum*, of trying to sell it. I wanted to reach people differently – I longed for a public that was just there, ready and curious and invested. I wanted to **share** the project, not **sell** it.

Drum ended up being successful and extremely satisfying, but the process of bringing it to an audience was alienating and disappointing. I was confused by the publicity which often described something "other" than what we were making, and I was relieved that the show gained traction through word of mouth. Once the show opened, we were no longer solely in charge of explaining the work. Critics were forced to be descriptive when talking about the show because it couldn't be categorized or compared to other works. Several critics couldn't help but describe the audience's behavior as well. Because once the show was open to the public, a public gathered around it. It was as if the audience themselves were part of the show.

This show was a major turning point for me. The audience was unlike any I had experienced before; I could feel their reactions to the show. There was something palpable happening, and I could comprehend that we had a public. The show was loud, it was raucous, it was feminist, it was queer. It drew a crowd, many of whom enjoyed the fruits of the long arduous work it took to make it. It also drew a *fruity audience*. Making *Drum* elicited a desire to make explicitly queer work and to name it as such. I recognized, for the first time, a deep need to reach more directly toward my personal and political investments.

During this same time Jess, Laryssa, Laura, and I took the opportunity to create a smaller group within the company, the Dyke Division of Two-headed Calf. This lesbian/trans faction of the *Drum* project began simultaneously creating a new queer project as we were premiering *Drum* in NYC. This new project was *Room for Cream*: the live lesbian serial drama.

We wanted to make queer work, but we also just wanted to work differently – more quickly, with less precision and more camp. We dreamed up a drama and wrote a script with versions of us as the main characters and the core cast. We previewed the live episode at a queer performance night at the *Poetry Project*, then made a teaser that we performed at a *Catch*[3] event. From that work, we felt we could make the world and the show. We began by establishing some parameters. These were that we rehearsed on Thursdays and we put up a new show every other Saturday; we wrote each script between Sunday and the following Wednesday; we did the tech for the show an hour before we opened the house; and we built narrative arcs around the availability of the actors and special guest performers. We approached La Mama with our loose, fly-by-the-seat-of-our-pants plan, in hopes of a space or support; and they said YES. They agreed to let us perform in the club theater at 5 pm – not a typical time for Saturday shows. This added another condition: we always performed on the sets of whatever show was booked in the club that evening.

We opened Episode One, on January 12, 2008 at 5 pm in the afternoon with a cast of 10. The theater was packed with queers, artists, and downtown luminaries. We had only sent out one e-mail blast; otherwise we used word of mouth (social media was not *the thing* yet). We began writing the next script the following day. Not only did audiences show up, but tickets became immediately scarce. It didn't take long before the audiences insinuated themselves into positions of authority; they claimed power over the project – their investments were palpable in the room. We found ourselves writing toward the energies and desires they fed to us. It was fantastic to not have to promote the show to some imaginary audience, to not have to convince them why they should show up. They wanted to show up, had demands and desires, and felt ownership.

This was the moment of my finally doing being a queer auteur director.

Publics and Counterpublics, or Individuals in Collision

(Stage Direction: Imagine. You're turning onto a block in New York City and are approaching a theater and seeing a crowd of people milling around on the street. The crowd is made of groups of friends, couples, people on first dates, artists, downtown theater luminaries, and a lone lover coming to see her girlfriend perform. You enter the lobby. Moving into the crowd you are aware of a tension building: Who gets let into the theater first? How do you get the best seats? Why aren't there lines? Over to your left are the people on the waitlist. You know from what happened at the last show that they are willing to stand at the back or sit on the aisle steps (or if they're lucky on a lap). Alas, a lesbian celebrity shows up demanding a ticket – she is "a friend of one of the artists!" It is so exciting, already, to be surrounded by people you actually find sexy. When you listen closely you hear people describing plot points and recreating last week's cliff hanger. They are creating a picture of the characters – who is sleeping with whom. "But don't worry" they promise their friends, "you don't have to know anything at all." The show will make enough sense; plot isn't the point. What they don't say, but what you all feel is that what truly matters is you: you are the event. It has already begun and you feel seen. For the next hour, you are inside an experience that is made for you – or at least with you in mind – you are the norm.)

This playful proposal, this live lesbian drama made manifest by a handful of queers, arose from a collective desire (how did they know so many people wanted this?) and that desire came to life in a small over-crowded room with a stage at its center. That was *Room for Cream*.

It wasn't until we made the live lesbian soap opera *Room for Cream* explicitly for a lesbian and queer audience that I was able to comprehend the unpredictable force of the audience as a co-author. These audiences had an unusually rogue and demanding presence that arose from a coupling of both resistance to and insistence on a shared identification. I was provoked and confronted in my role as the director. This experience forced me to look hard at the assumptions I made about how a theatrical work affects its audience and compelled me to relearn what was possible in theater, or at least what was possibly interesting.

Before those encounters, I had a kind of arrogance, a blind faith in my own skill set. I proceeded as if my sophisticated understanding of how to use space, how to work with actors, how to engage design as language, and how to analyze a script allowed me to perform a kind of magic on the audience. In retrospect, this deep reliance on "know how," on craft, and on the so-called skills of the trade was just another form of passing. I'm a nuts and bolts director, I can play by the rules, and I can fit in. Passing is survival, but passing with gusto is success. However, embracing my positionality, a queer director making work for a queer audience, changed everything. Here the conditions inside the "room" exposed the radical possibilities of coming together around a performance and made manifest a kind of feedback loop. This feedback loop is enabled by a counterpublic in the sense that Michael Warner elaborates in *Publics and Counterpublics*. Warner writes:

> Like all publics, a counterpublic comes into being through an address to indefinite strangers…But counterpublic discourse also addresses those strangers as being not just anybody. Addressees are socially marked by their participation in this kind of discourse; ordinary people are presumed to not want to be mistaken for the kind of person who would participate in this kind of talk or be present in this kind of scene.[4]

In an earlier elaboration, the brilliant theorist José Esteban Muñoz identified disidentification as a particularly queer strategy of survival and resistance: one "that works within and outside the dominant public sphere simultaneously."[5] While embracing the expansive permissions afforded by strategies of disidentification for minoritarian artists, the experience of being in the room of any number of queer performance events suggests other operations than those offered by the binary force of identification or disidentification. I am interested in the ways in which queer directors, queer theater, and performance artists striving for strategies beyond survival reach their audience on a "cellular level" – pushing inside and underneath identity toward audiences and spectators who are inconsistent, unpredictable, and reactive. Something happens in the encounters of performance – something explosive or disarming or comforting, or possibly satiating, that interjects into the co-inhabitation of space the messy consequences of overlapping experiences, emotions, and connections that collide and ignite the room into a disparate shared experience and that allows for our witnessing of each other.

Producing Politics and Good Theater

The conditions of the project *Room for Cream,* a performance event/space I co-created and conceived *for* a predominately lesbian and queer audience, contradicted all things that conventionally constitute "good" or "professional" theater. And, indeed, many theater people outright rejected the work despite the fact that it was wildly popular, constantly sold out, had a dream-team of artistic collaborators, and an energy and force that could be felt in the room. When I say the work refused conventional standards, I am not suggesting that it was amateur, but rather that something altogether different was going on in the space of the work that had everything to do with the audience and their active production of its meaning. *Room for Cream* cannot be understood by looking *only* at the script, or considering the acting and making sense of the "stage picture." Something happened in the space of the event, and, even though our creative team could not totally understand what it was, we were constantly reacting to it and increasingly accountable to it. I was a primary creator of *Room for Cream* (directing and acting in all 27 episodes and being one of five script writers) and I was acutely aware that, from the moment the project met its public, the project was no longer ours. Rather the work was being made in the moment of performance – with an audience that came together in a desire to produce culture and, I would assert, politics.

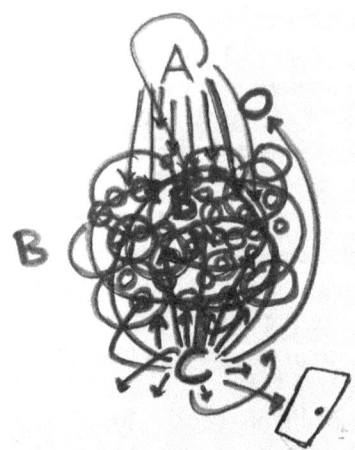

FIGURE 1.2   Sketch by O'Harra of *How a play is experienced.*

This coming together, as a public or counterpublic, as performers and as audience, allows us to appear to each other in both action and speech. Philosopher Hannah Arendt asserts that this a unique human capability that is at the foundation of politics or political work. Primary to the relations in the theater is a desire to appear before each other, what Arendt calls an "urge towards self-display."[6] (She elaborates on these conditions of action and praxis at length in her book *The Human Condition* and continues in *The Life of the Mind.*)

Imagine that this is a sketch of how a play is experienced (Figure 1.2):

How the director influences, sculpts, and creates is always in collaboration with others: the event of the play/the performance (A) inhabits a space with the audience (C) so that (B) can happen. To read this sketch imagine that section A is the play or the performance work, section C is the audience or public who gather in the room to experience the work, and B is what happens in that encounter.

Section A is all the things that make the performance – the play, the actors, the set, the dramaturgy, the directing, the space, the political moment, etc. It is the culmination of all the work the artistic team has done being performed in real time for an audience.

Section C is the audience. These are people. They have desires. They are also caught up in their own lives, even as they are sitting in the theater. They are also members of publics, many publics; and, whether or not they acknowledge their affiliation with said publics, these belongings certainly inform how they arrive at the theater on any given evening.

(Stage direction: Look at section C – the audience. I made this sketch several times in a notebook, and my daughter found it and asked me what that was supposed to mean. I explained that the arrows represent the places where an audience member's focus might be directed while they were watching a play. She felt that she could do a better drawing of this idea. I asked her to try. My daughter drew the door to show you that some people in the audience are thinking about things that are outside of the room. Which is true. That is also happening.)

Section B is totally elusive and singular. It may or may not be recognized as it is happening and may or may not be articulable afterwards. It definitely is not fixed. It is an infinite set of colliding experiences. But it is also the site of action and of politics (Figure 1.3).

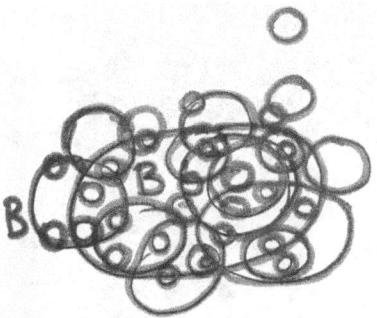

FIGURE 1.3   Sketch by O'Harra of *How the audience receives information.*

A central aspect of the work of the director is to interrogate and continually address what happens at that moment of encounter between a work and its audience. Imagine all of the bubbles as what places where the audience and show are in relation – are making meaning together. Some bubbles are big, some overlap each other, some are contained in one another – while some are almost by themselves on the edge of the central bubble. This togetherness and lack of total cohesion is the space of collision.

The Making of Meaning

This moment of making meaning in real time with your audience does not necessarily need to be relegated solely to the unpredictable but should be an intentional appeal to make shared experiences. Or so you would hope. Can directors build practices or make choices, at each phase of their process, that influence or expand the conversation that compels the public to gather in self-display and meet the production as co-author? This question drives what I consider to be the active research of any queer auteur director.

This is a question I arrived at in this research as praxis project *I'm Bleeding All Over the Place*. In the fourth part, I directed much of my focus toward this specific question. I made a performance, disguised as a tour, in which the audience was led through a play: spatially, textually, and temporally. *A Living History Tour,* the subtitle of this event, attempted to stage both the conflict in and the desire for a deep connection between the director and her audience – or more specifically a director's desire to understand their relationship to making the performance meaningful or impactful.

In one scene, members of the audience are led into a small space to sit across from an actor. Each actor speaks the same monolog at roughly the same time but delivers it intimately to the one or two audience members who gather in front of them (Figure 1.4).

*** *Curtains are pulled down to divide the space into ten lanes. Each actor is isolated with one or two audience members. And although the audience sees only one actor – the ten actors speak this monologue in unison – you can hear them all.*

(**The monologue is about 6 minutes long and ends with the following:**)

All Actors: (*simultaneously*).

I'm gonna tell you something I think you know already. I memorized *these* lines too. We all did. We're playing. You are not. Or is that true? Here's a fact for you. Or maybe it's a philosophical argument. Just like me, you **Appear** and therefore have an

FIGURE 1.4 Photo of *I'm Bleeding All Over the Place: A living history tour* at La Mama E.T.C. 2017 photo by Julieta Cervantes.

Urge towards **Self-Display**. I'm an actor. I'm doing something to you with my perfor-mance, but you're creating this too. *(pause)* Nice costume. *(Smile – like with recogni-tion or compassion)* Look. . . It's not actually us who are talking to you. **We** wouldn't say any of this. **Brooke** would. She did. Brooke O'Harra wrote these words in front of a woodstove in Portland, Maine on January 12, 2016. She was reading Hannah Arendt and writing this script and she lost track of me—us *(indicating to other ac-tors)*—she was too busy thinking about you. She's been thinking about you this whole time. But Brooke can't be here with you. Only I can. She can **direct** all she wants, but she can't control this. She can't respond to you. . . to You.

She'd probably disapprove of that costume you are wearing. And she wouldn't like what you're doing with your face.

And you have no presence.

See. See what she's doing to us? You know what this is? It's provocation.

It's okay. Don't resist. Just think whatever you're thinking. That's part of this. Or feel what you're feeling. . .Hold on to that. Keep it. Here. With us. In this place right here between me and you. This is our encounter. Make meaning. Make meaning. Make meaning with me. Make meaning with me.[7]

The impulse here is to reach through the actor and address the audience directly and to bring some material shape to the tense and potent encounter between a spectator and a work. Perhaps, it is a balm for an unrelenting ambivalence I have observed among my queer and feminist colleagues and friends toward making theater.

My ambivalence is not so much with the theater itself as an art but more with this persistent conservatism of this contemporary moment in theater (particularly in what we call the *American Theater*). I am distrustful of the institutions that produce and support the theater and of programs in theater education that train practitioners to make theater.

As is always the case with ambivalence, there is a core desire that is blocked from its potential fulfillment. We want to be in a room together. We want to make meaning together. But how do expansive encounters between queer makers and their unpredictable and unruly publics survive the interventions of a field that refuses to budge or make room for their desires? In other words: How do I, as a queer auteur director, make work in this field? Or, as is the point of this book, how do *you* do it?

(Stage Direction: Admit it. You're a little excited by that idea too. You feel a desire to find a place where our investments and interests or fears collide, intersect, or maybe even, repulse each other. That's a kind of liveness that must be possible. Answer this. What is possible in the space between me and you? What happens when other people are involved? Playwrights, actors, designers? Whose is the voice? Do you feel your own voice in the theater no matter your role in the process? Why the theater? Why that room? What makes the stage explosive with possibility? Could it be more possible?)

To return again to Arendt: praxis or action is fragile, unpredictable, unresolved, never done in isolation and never completed. Action presupposes a plurality in which individuals are both equal and distinct. She provocatively asserts that action initiates a story that is, importantly, authorless as multiple people and multiple forces coexist and impact the story unpredictably. Theater is a medium in which praxis is a foundational condition. These conditions allow for our work to be charged, political and seductive.

Working Inside and Outside of Structures

The director's work is tightly bound to the structures of the theater: the space itself, casting, working with actors, the language of stage design, scripts, etc. These relationships must be negotiated with enthusiasm and care. A director should not depend only on tools or tricks of the trade to navigate these collaborations.

We can take cues from great U.S. playwrights like Suzan-Lori Parks and Adrienne Kennedy who have managed to free themselves of the confines of arbitrary rules and codes. Kennedy and Parks even disavow the theater while continuing to write for the stage and for their audiences. They seem to find relief when discussing their shared discomfort in the theater and with the word playwright in this recorded conversation.

Adrienne Kennedy:	Very often I'm not in New York for the production period. I wasn't here when Joe Papp did my plays, I came for the last week. . . And when Ellen Stewart did my plays, I never went to rehearsals. Seth Allen didn't even want me to come – I worked a lot with Joe Chaikin when we first did *A Movie Star Has to Star in Black and White*. . . . I love being a writer – but I can't say I love being a playwright.
Suzan-Lori Parks:	Why?
Adrienne Kennedy:	I feel that God gave me a gift to create what I call "little scenes," I really mean that, I'm not trying to denigrate them. I can create little

	scenes on paper. But I always found getting involved in a production very difficult and often a tremendous let-down.
Suzan-Lori Parks:	Being in rehearsals isn't my favorite thing either. I'm not a "theater person." Some people love it, but. . .
Adrienne Kennedy:	That's exactly how I feel.[8]

Parks may not be a "theater person," but she is one of America's greatest playwrights. She also writes essays about writing plays that push against the core assumptions of what can happen on a stage. Adrienne Kennedy is one of only five playwrights in the Norton Anthology of Literature, which includes her play *A Movie Star Has to Star in Black and White*.

(Stage Direction: Get up and do a little dance in celebration of that. Give thanks to the genius who slipped that amazing and complicated play into that funny educational canon.)

Despite their success, Parks and Kennedy are black women writing in a field that for much of their careers has been dominated by a white, patriarchal, heteronormative gaze. I wonder if it is because their position is outside this gaze, or is it that they have been scrutinized for so long by a gaze that doesn't see them that they can so brilliantly refuse it. They toss norms aside, skip rehearsals if they want, and delve directly into the live event – presenting texts on the stage that demand that audiences find a relation to them. But maybe it is also because they are playwrights that they can take permission to be radical.

Consider the playwright Maria Irene Fornes, a groundbreaking queer writer who made every play into an experiment of form. She, like many writers who pushed the *American Theater* toward experimentation and growth, preferred to direct her own work. Playwrights Julia Jarcho, Tina Satter, Young Jean Lee, John Jesurun, and Richard Maxwell also direct their own work. This is not because they are first and foremost directors, but because directors often rely explicitly on tools and craft; and this dependence tempers or blocks their access to experimental writing – so, instead of working with the writing, they work against it. They try to squeeze the work into parameters that the playwright has bypassed or ignored completely. Directors can become easily bogged down by their own (or their producer's) insistence and reliance on the tools of the trade and their misguided training in *Poetics* (*Yes, get me started on* Poetics!!) while many contemporary playwrights have found a way to free their work up from festering formulas. This is mostly because the most exciting MFA playwriting programs are run by experimental writers while directors are still taught that they are craftspeople and that they must adhere to a strict process. As this divide in theater education grows, it causes frustration for playwrights who need and want someone to champion and guide their work toward production.

Although directors are often seen as "interpretative" artists, they are, of course, makers who engage space, text, and performers – from a distinct role, one that is profoundly different from that of the playwright. The vision of a given performance and its realization are so clearly a product of the personal collisions engendered by and through collaboration: the collaboration among the creative team as well as that between those people and the histories that precede them, the culture that engulfs them, and the context in which they address an audience or public. As a queer auteur director, considering the work of the director through these tensions helps me to "make something happen" between the event of the show and the audience who are there for it.

To do this, we must investigate a series of important questions: How do we wrest our work from institutional imperatives of public-building and culture-building and return to an artist-driven discourse that engages the unique concerns of the artists and their publics in this moment? How do we make "play" and activate all relationships, whether among artists in the rehearsal room or between the production and the audience?

Wanting

This is what I wish could happen when I go to a theater:

I wish there was popcorn at plays.

I wish that every seat was a good seat.

I wish the actors didn't tell me or show me how to feel.

I wish I could sometimes get a cold IPA, preferably on tap and in a glass, so I wouldn't have to worry about single use plastics.

I wish I could discover something right there in that room with those people.

I wish I didn't have to see people's screens. But it would be nice if people could share their experience in real time, if they wanted. Because that is a thing these days.

I wish ideas weren't precious, but that they were meaningful.

I wish people didn't come to the play "just because" they had tickets or their kid was in it, and then say they didn't like it because it wasn't "their thing," Those people should have made other plans.

I wish I could get up and leave if I wasn't having a good experience.

I wish all the actors were gender queer and that the gender of the characters separated from the actors and floated in the atmosphere of the theater like an aroma.

I wish a stranger sitting next to me wasn't afraid to make noise or might even turn to me with some emphatic exclamation of disbelief or awe or rage.

I wish there wasn't a subscriber audience and that the director was an auteur.

I wish, if the play was about issues that didn't affect me directly (or about an experience that I stand outside of), that the audience would mostly be people for whom the story was being told. And, whether or not I was implicated in the play, and even if I was totally irrelevant to the concerns, I could be in a room with the people who the play was for and that I would have to reckon with my relevance or irrelevance. And that nobody would have to feel responsible for me.

I wish there weren't any black outs and that the actors didn't always remember their lines and that there weren't blue outs with actors in period costume running around hiding props and moving furniture, and that the preshow music wasn't misguided and generally coopting someone else's culture.

I wish only children went to the theater. Or only queers. Or only church ladies in special Sunday hats who talked back to the actors, even though it was kind of distracting and disruptive.

I wish that going to the theater could encompass all of these possibilities but not all at once and that we could expect this kind of diversity and that we could feel so overwhelmed by the possibility of what might happen in the room that we go into the theater ready for something or for anything.

I wish we could even be scared to go to the theater, but in a good way. Or that we could just say, "maybe I'll skip that one," and then we just skip it.

Notes

1 Ariel Goldberg, "A Routine Obsession," in *The Estrangement Principle* (New York: Nightboat Books, 2016), 6.
2 Ibid., 5.
3 *Catch* was an evening length event held in various venues across NYC that highlighted the work of performance makers as they were in progress of developing new shows. It was curated by Andrew Dinwiddie, Caleb Hammons, and Jeff Larson and was hosted by numerous venues in NYC as well as some out-of-town events in Minneapolis and Philadelphia. It was started in 2003 by Jenny Seastone-Stern at a Williamsburg arts space and bar called Galapagos. Each event was numbered – the last event was in July of 2017 and was *Catch 74*.
4 Michael Warner, "Publics and Counterpublics," in *Public Culture* (Duke University Press, Volume 14, Number 1, Winter 2002), 86.
5 José Esteban Muñoz, *Disidentifications: Queers of Color and the Performance of Politics* (Minneapolis and London: University of Minnesota Press, 1999), 5.
6 Hannah Arendt, "One / Thinking," in *The Life of the Mind* (San Diego, New York and London: A Harvest Book, Harcourt, Inc., 1978), 21.
7 Brooke O'Harra with Casey Llewellyn, *I'm Bleeding All Over the Place: A Living History Tour* (Performance Script, New York, 2016_not published), 18–9.
8 Suzan-Lori Parks, "Adrienne Kennedy," in *Suzan-Lori Parks in Person* edited by Philip C Kolin and Harvey Young (London and New York: Routledge, 2014), 59. Note on *I'm Bleeding All Over the Place:* This study is the product of a series of active research-based collaborations with numerous artists: curator and scholar Johanna Burton; playwright and actor Heidi Schreck; playwright and actor Kristen Kosmas; playwright Erin Courtney; director and playwright John Jesurun; playwright, director, and actor Jeff Weiss; artist Sadie Benning; artist Moyra Davies; performer and director Kate Valk; playwright Casey Llewellyn; performer and artist J.D. Stokely; the poet Ross Gay and the new music ensemble Yarn/Wire.

CARD CATALOG

During the first three nights (encounters) of the performance as research project *I'm Bleeding All Over the Place: Studies in directing or nine encounters between me and you,* I had the lights up on the audience and passed out notecards they could write on as the performance was happening. The audience was given the option to keep their cards throughout the performance or pass them along to people seated near them, so they could ostensibly be in dialogue with other audience members in real time. At the end of the event, the audience returned the notecards to me. Each night we used a different color card; this way I could tell which notes came from which performance. The audience were asked not to put their names on the cards. Over the three encounters, we collected approximately 170 cards. They had a lot to reveal. The overriding theme was the audience's self-awareness as participants in the event and their willingness to be explicit about their own desires. When I say participants, I do not mean that the audience felt involved in participatory theater but that they recognized their own role in the creation of value. Some were willing to aggressively interrogate their experience. There was also an interesting balance between those who owned or took responsibility for their experience and those who demanded that the experience meet their (unspoken) needs and desires.

DOI: 10.4324/9781003253402-2

Here is a handful of scans of the notes:

EXAMPLE 1

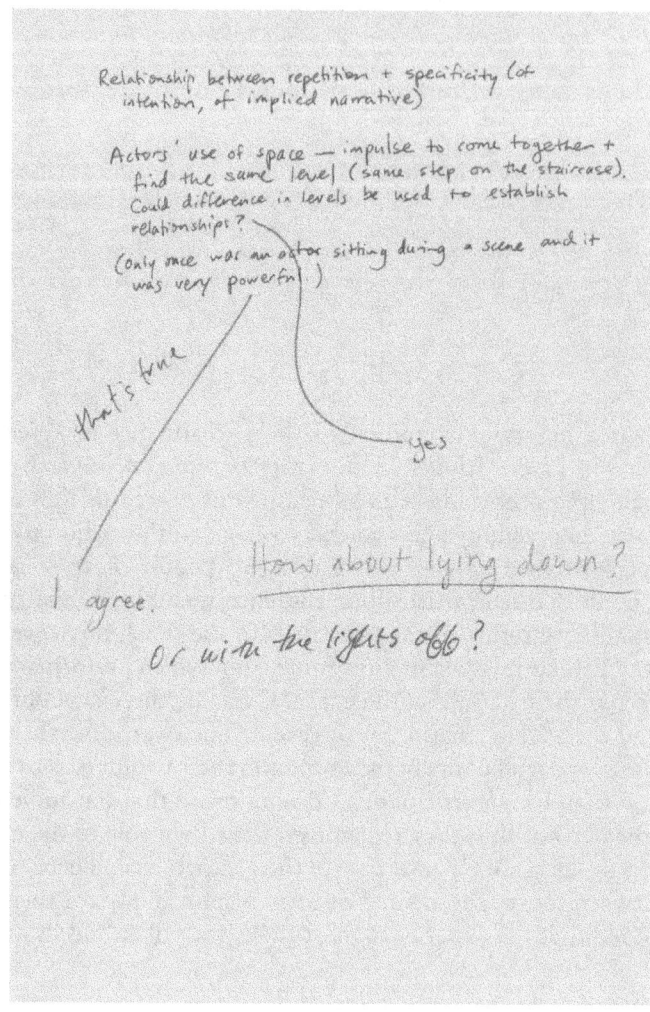

EXAMPLE 2

Tell the story, anyway you want   PIZZA   shards

DIY PLAYWRITING   FORMING Narrative

I could go on and on

TRY THEM DIFFERENT WAYS

HARD TO READ THEM   OR

how can acting not
be a fill in the blank
(of the director's or playwright's
intentions) but

an autonomous art?

_____

Do it while pushing
the couche — lifting it —
carrying it around the Room!
/ (voice of Yvonne Rainer)

EXAMPLE 3

How important is it to understand early
that the dialogue is not tied
to a specific actor/character

How much rehearsal feels like
the installation of art work.

I Love
that idea

Yeah, kind of wrong to be an 'audience'
of it. But it's hard to have an audience-feeling
w/o an audience.

"CAN YOU GUYS TELL WHICH ONES
ARE REALLY FROM OUR LIVES?"

EXAMPLE 4

I came back for the second
day. I realized upon walking
in that I have no expectations.
It's as though I wasn't here
before.
I think you've opened up
~~a~~ a transgressive, or maybe I mean
challenging, and generous space.
So generous! It ~~gives~~ and gives,
maybe to the point of
transgression...?

† I always want to punch
that guy in the face ~~too~~.

Wow, the lack of affect
in your delivery, compared
to the actors is immense,
bilo metric! how different
the experience of hearing these
things ~~~~ is.

EXAMPLE 5

BEST ATMOSPHERE I'VE EVER FELT IN THIS SPACE

I DON'T KNOW JEFF WEISS. WOULD I BE LESS SEDUCED/CHARMED
W/OUT THE INVITATIONAL TIMBRE OF IN INTRO? W/OUT
THIS ATMOSPHERE? I FEEL LIKE YOU SLIPPED ME A DRINK.

YOU ASK ME TO IGNORE VENUE, BUT IT IS HARD. SOME THEATER
TROPES — 2 PPL SPEAKING SIMULTANEOUSLY (OR CITATICALLY) —
FEEL LIKE REFERENCES HERE, A STAGING OF THEATER AND
NOT "JUST" (NATURALIZED) THEATER.

"WHAT R U DOING TONIGHT?" : I WAS @ THE WRITING YESTERDAY.
MY DAR DANIAN HAVE THIS VIDEO THAT — OH SHIT NEVER
MIND. LAUGHED TO HATE.

Singing is always emotional.
And "everyday" is some way —
but not the way people
mean w/the everyday" —

Essay Two

BRINGS US TOGETHER AND KEEPS US APART

I have been directing, making work, and thinking about theater for almost 30 years. I have been teaching acting and directing for 20 years. Each morning I wake up feeling dykier, faggier, and queerer than the day before. I wake up thinking about yeses and resistance – good and bad – and translating resistance back into yeses and possibility and potential. As Eve Kosofsky Sedgwick writes in *Tendencies*,

> I think many adults (and I am among them) are trying, in our work, to keep faith with vividly remembered promises made to ourselves in childhood: promises to make invisible possibilities and desires visible; to make the tacit things explicit; to smuggle queer representation in where it must be smuggled and, with the relative freedom of adulthood, to challenge queer-eradicating impulses frontally where they are to be so challenged.[1]

I try to meet this challenge by giving my practice a name, like calling myself a queer auteur director; by having faith in our relations and our perversions; and by allowing that transgressions are generous.

Let us wake up tomorrow, all of us, as queer auteur directors. Even you, the imposter, you too will rise in the morning as a queer auteur. We can begin this transformation by attending to and tending our relationships, starting with our audience. *Never mind that they are elusive, haunting, unstable, unwieldy, and demanding!* By shifting our focus toward the audience and the conditions of our encounters, we can alter the landscapes of this profession, sometimes known as theater. I propose we do so in these ways:

we repurpose the terms of/in our vocabulary
we reclaim our spaces
we grant ourselves permission to imagine our publics

DOI: 10.4324/9781003253402-3

Renegotiating Vocabulary

Over time, theater has amassed a vast vocabulary and with it a plethora of conceits.

Can I ask you to do something? Take one minute to compile the first terms that come to mind when you think of theater vocabulary. Jot them down somewhere.

This is what I came up with: actor, character, props, downstage, sets, entrances, lights up and down, cues, beats, actions, French scenes!, sightlines, quick-changes, wings, spike marks, three-quarter-stance, and scenic painting. I doubt our lists are the same. But I imagine yours, like mine, has a kind of haphazard quality.

This is because the theater is a haphazard kind of technology, compounding and adding technical aspects and giving language to an array of coded choices. This "technology" rarely discards its excess. While some features of the theater have been discarded (*like the prompter!*), for the most part what we use now is a vast accumulation of (uninterrogated) terms. I mean terms as both the conditions of choice-making and the vocabulary that names those conditions.

GAZR

Take, for example, the story of GAZR, the fictional poet-turned-rapper. A few years ago, I was helping James Allister Sprang, a young Black artist who makes performance, prepare his work to show during the Association of Presenters and Producers (APAP) conference in New York. James is an artist who employs poetry, sound, performance, photography, and all sorts of other things in his work. He did not go to school for theater, he went to school for art; but some of his work crosses over with theater, and he received a "commission" to develop one of these crossover works, as GAZR, through a residency for the *Under the Radar Festival*. By saying yes to the show (three performances in repertory with other works by different artists), James plunked down into the world of theater and its disorienting vocabulary. What does it mean to "rep" it, to strike it? What's a rep plot? A TD? The folks from *Under the Radar* sent James a ground plan of the stage on which he was scheduled to perform, and the drawing of the stage (set in a black box) had wavy lines on three sides of it. James was like, "What is that?" And I was like, "I guess those are blacks." And he was like, "Blacks?" and I was like, "Yeah, theater blacks. . .black curtains." And he asked, "Why? Why is a curtain in front of the wall? Why am I boxed in by heavy black curtains?" And I explained the conceit as I understood it, "Because they're *invisible*," then I said, "Because they are *neutral*." And he was like, "All right, I guess GAZR is going to be surrounded by invisible blacks."

Heavy black curtains aren't the only *invisible* things in the theater. Theater is reliant on ideas of invisibility. They have used the practice of pretending not to see what is right in front of them for so long that they have come to depend on it as a kind of band-aid or lazy solution for larger issues like inequity. You only need to consider "color-blind" casting to understand the limitations of this impulse. What is color-blind casting? It refers to a practice where, in a production, actors of any race are cast as the characters in a play regardless of whether the play was written for a mixed race cast – the assumption being that we do not see race as part of the story. This is a reasonable practice to build opportunities for performers who otherwise have had very few roles available to them. And the practice is now being used in contemporary serialized dramas to great success. But the problem is when color-blind casting becomes a convenient solution to the very large problem the theater has with racial and gender equity. And it exposes the theater's blasé ideas about invisibility and erasure. This impulse for imagining away things that are right in front of us is embedded in the aesthetics, technologies, and vocabulary of theater.

Even the most benign conceits in the theater impact practical choices we make in regard to aesthetics and to time and to movement in space. Often the things deemed invisible are kind of quirky. But as soon as you question them (either their validity or their necessity), lines get drawn.

Spike Marks

Take, for example, spike marks, the little strips of colored tape (sometimes it even glows) that mark up a stage floor so the actors and/or tech team know where to place furniture and other objects. Many designers choose, right before a show opens, to paint over them so you see only the impressions of the tape on the stage floor. But even when the spike marks aren't glowing or highly visible, their use triggers strange physical behavior on stage. The stage hand or actor is often caught staring at the floor fussing with an inch here or there. Transitions become unnecessarily protracted. The spike marks alter the relationship of bodies to both space and time; there is no fluidity in seeking out spike marks. Spike marks do one thing: they allow for the exact placement of furniture and bodies in space, but achieving that perfection may affect both bodies and movement in space and what we see on the floor – meaning their use should be conditional and negotiable.

I could attempt to recreate the conversations I have had with technical directors, production managers, and stage managers about why I don't want to use spike marks. I could tell you about their incredulity about my insistence that the actors have a good enough idea of where they or some piece of furniture goes at any given moment – after all they're only negotiating a 30 by 20-foot space. I could tell you about how they find it shocking that it bothers me that the marks are visible or that the act of seeking spike marks forces a strange texture of movement on the stage. But probably you can already imagine how disruptive this request is to the business of theater – spike marks are HOW IT IS DONE! *What about finding their lights? What about safety?!!!*

Refusing spike marks is not seen as a legitimate choice made by a member of the team. Rather, it makes you into someone who is negligent, someone who undermines the systems. Is this request truly dangerous? Or are aesthetic concerns, concerns about movement and time, the concerns of some slaphappy queer auteur who has no regard for the rules? Perhaps that is truly what is dangerous.

This may seem like an inane example. They're just spike marks. But, know this, queer auteur, the problem is not with the little strips of tape, but with your banal request that is met with fierce hostility. The problem is the way the *professionals* dig in, lines are drawn, and norms are protected. The problem is in how easily you become a threat. To further be a menace here, I will make this question bold: **What and who are threatened when we allow the very thing which everyone is trying to pretend does not exist to be visible?**

Sightlines

Consider the sightline. To begin, I will state what we all know: not everyone in the audience of a performance has the same view. A sightline describes what an individual spectator can see of a performance from a particular spot in the architectural space of the theater. Sightlines vary depending on where one is seated or standing. Some are genuinely better than others; some are obstructed; some are just straight-up funky. Some theaters adjust seat pricing to account for these differences, and some theaters place the onus on the audience to resolve these inequities using the first come first serve approach; those who want better seats have to show up early.

What do sightlines reveal about the culture of our performance spaces? They teach me that inequality is built into the structure that not everyone deserves or is expected to experience the work as it is conceived, and that discomfort and obstruction is acceptable.

The Term Theater

We should take stock of the relationships between the physical space and the "terms of the space." The theater exists as a space that physically defines relations between a performance and its audience. It is a room. A theater is also a commercial entity or a not-for-profit that is managed, and the theater is also an art form. You might make theater in a theater run by a theater.

The physical space, the power structures, and the art are deeply entangled. The "terms" of the art are bound up in the space itself, the stage, the liveness, and the parameters. These terms are derived from both the real physical space and from ideas maintained and formed by systems of power and structure built around, and in relation to, these physical spaces.

The terms of theater are so commonplace in the rehearsal room and in production meetings that using them is often a rite of passage. Using them also makes you believe that your command of this vocabulary translates to a command of the art and even allows you to assume that the audience reads these terms the same way. Neither is really true. Instead, this reliance on coded terms promotes a theater that is staid, robust with fakery, and exclusive.

This isn't a new idea. The conceits of the theater have always troubled the artists; this is why there is so much meta-theater. But recognizing this rub hasn't stopped us from relying on a great many assumptions about legibility. And it hasn't stopped those in power from using these terms to contain transgressors.

But you, who are now an army of queer auteurs, will flip this on its head. Because, instead of detesting these conceits, you might flirt with them; you will learn them and then navigate, twist, and undermine them. You can hide in these constraints, or you can expose the insides of the form. You have no choice but to operate inside, around, and outside of these terms. They are not just their terms, they are all of ours to use at will, with whimsy or even as weapons of our own.

The other thing you should remember is that not all people who attend the theater even comprehend these terms. They are not legible to all of your potential spectators.

There are people in your audience who become frustrated and confused by the assumptions of the theater. The terms of the theater are perplexing to them and quite often alienating. Unfortunately they typically do not speak up, instead they suffer the experience as an insult, they leave the show and choose not to return to the theater. And instead of acknowledging that this might be happening, most institutions cling to their terms or choose to "educate" their audiences with the help of dramaturgs.

Reclaim the Spaces

I want to be helpful to you queer auteurs, I want to offer up wonderful solutions for how exactly you can make these spaces your own and make them bend to your will. I want you to see what has been made invisible by suggestion or neglect so you can point to it and say, "It's right there!"

Like most directors, I conceive of myself as a problem solver. But what we need, all of us, is potential and possibility. But potential and possibility are not problems, they cannot be solved. This isn't tidy work because potential and possibility thrive in conditions of instability and ambiguity. Or maybe just openness.

Questions

I'll take a moment and share an anecdote. It's about Merce Cunningham the choreographer who, when I first met him, told me an anecdote about a babysitter who taught him ballet in her kitchen and who walked on her hands with a giant rubber band around her skirt and maybe she was even smoking a cigarette. *Is this true?* Anyhow, this babysitter was the person who made Merce Cunningham a dancer. I'm not sure who made me a director, but when I was 19 I was given a responsibility, which now I understand was a gift, which was to be host and guide to Cunningham during a week-long visit to the college I was attending. I met him each morning and walked him to his engagements; and when I didn't have class, I would hang out while he spoke to classes or rehearsed with his dancers. It was a pretty perfunctory role. But it changed me. And what changed me was so simple – it was watching Merce work. When he worked with his dancers, he watched, and he asked questions. He would notice something that needed adjustment or better coordination; and, instead of telling the dancers what to do, he asked them what was happening? What did they think they were doing? How might they adjust? What could be different? He only asked questions.

I think Cunningham used questions as a way of saying yes to what was possible or to the potential of the dancers to give voice and body to their own experience. Or, maybe questions shut down the possibility of saying no.

The idea of saying yes is quite radical. On the surface it seems easy. Yes means go. Yes is confirmation. But who gets to say yes or no? That person, the yes or no man, has power. If you are a parent, you will not question this statement. You say "no" because you are heading off a disaster, you say "no" because you know something your kid doesn't know yet. And when you say "yes," well, what a gift! – that extra TV show, reading for a half hour more before they have to turn off the lights. You are generous, you are flexible, you have no energy to argue – whatever. You have power and you believe that you wield it for the protection or betterment of your child and your household. But why do institutions and granting organizations exert this kind of power (parental power) over artists? They have power because of the scarcity of resources. They have resources, and you don't.

This kind of paternalistic control that resourced institutions, funders, and their gatekeepers assume over artists is dangerous to artistic practices. It insists that people with money control cultural production, not artists. And, unfortunately, it is the norm. Ask anyone.

Watchdogs, or My Complaint against the Dramaturg

For a couple of decades, theaters and funders have begun to protect their interests or investments through a seemingly innocuous gatekeeper called a dramaturg.

Dramaturgs have been installed in institutions in the role of intermediaries, they are hired by institutions to "support" and "help" a work come to fruition. But what has happened is that they have become a fixture that more often than not intervenes on behalf of the institutions by protecting and upholding norms and by protecting ideas that are old and staid in the theater. And whether or not this is intentional, they are slowing the progress of theater; in holding on so tightly to an older, whiter, and more traditional theater audience, these in-house dramaturgs are tempering artists' potential and power.

You might question what this looks like. In theory, dramaturgy is the research that supports the practice of a writer, a director, or even an actor before and during the process of developing a script, production, or character. But the dramaturg that works for a producer often becomes a meddler. Under the guise of "caring for the play" they suggest revisions that "clarify" the narrative; they ask that cuts be made or even ask that you write an additional monologue for a character to, perhaps, explain themselves in some way. This is often with the hope that the play comes in at around 90 minutes. Not all narrative should be clarified. Not all stories should be tidy. Some plays could be and should be 50 minutes, while others might need to be 4 hours long. All of this meddling is bound up in this idea that the dramaturg is some kind of conduit to the audience that they somehow know better what an audience wants or what a "script needs." But why does this person have this power and what makes them so profoundly knowledgeable that they can assert that they know better than the playwright, the directors, and all the other folks in the rehearsal room?

Just recently, some dear friends of mine were working on a new play in an off-broadway theater. They were all known for their skills and brilliance as experimental artists. And as they came to a place in the process where the play was staged and rehearsed, where sets and lights were in, and the artists in the room were feeling like now the actors can really work and listen and hone their choices, all of a sudden the dramaturg (also the literary manager) stepped into the room and started suggesting edits and big changes. According to them, they were helping to clarify the story, change the pace, and whatever else. This is not what the creative team needed. The actors needed to build on their work with one another, and the director and playwright needed to step back and watch and listen. Instead, in came the meddler claiming to protect the play while sabotaging the process. The actors grew frustrated and didn't feel comfortable (they were working in front of a preview audience); they grew upset at the director; the playwright couldn't really step back enough to see her play with all the incessant tinkering from outside; and the director lost control of the rhythms she was building. And she also couldn't sit back and watch the play. There was a kind of collapse of morale and of vision. The process had been coopted by this person (this dramaturg) who had the false idea that it was the text itself that was what needed protection and nurture. And by hailing the text as the only true voice, they trampled on the work and art of the people who were in the room. It, also, was just really bad timing inside of the process.

Why did this happen? And, more importantly, why does this happen so frequently?

For many of you, you might be wondering if this is really true? Who are these folks? Well, the Literary Manager and Dramaturgs of America website describes the role of dramaturgs this way: "In the ecology of theatre-making, dramaturgs and literary managers forge a critical link between artists and institutions, and institutions and their communities."[2] Geoffrey Proehl, author of the books *Ghost Light: An Introductory Handbook to Dramaturgy* and *Towards a Dramaturgical Sensibility: Landscape and Journey,* uses the following phrases and words to describe dramaturgs: "historical, critical, literary, and philosophical consciousness," "watchdog," "audience's surrogate," "designated readers," "keeper of the text," "word person," and "diplomat or mediator."[3]

These words imply that the artist and their audience need an intermediary. Do they? Who and what is being protected?

What the dramaturg is trained to do is research. And research or the accumulation of knowledge about your material, your author, the context, history, etc., is absolutely necessary. But directors and playwrights should do their own research. They should digest the complexities of their materials. Research offers you fluency; it enables you to strive toward your impulses and nurture your work. It should support collaboration because you will enter the room having thought about the project in all of its context which puts you in a better place to listen. To give over these essential aspects of an artistic practice is to forgo potential and possibility. To allow someone to come in with an authority and claim to knowing what makes that project work for the audience undermines the people who have been in that room, who have a process of their own.

Who Says Yes?

More importantly, it is **your** curiosity and **your** investments that directly cultivate your relationship with your audience. It should not be so hard to just say yes. *Try it with me,* "Yes yes yes yes yes." But far too often we find our radical yeses outside of mainstream institutions. We are forced to seek other venues in order to thrive. This is what the downtown allows. It has been the fertile playspace of queer theater makers for decades.

This makes me think of the Spring of 1985 issue of *The Drama Review,* which was dedicated to what they called Pop Performance but referred to a whole array of performance events and practices that were happening in New York's East Village at the time, including experimental theater and dance. Many of the artists working in these spaces were queer and some have become very influential in the American Theater, like Robert Wilson and Lisa Kron. I like their work and I enjoy their success, but so many of the artists you were exposed to in a week in downtown NYC in 1984 are/were incredible: Carmelita Tropicana, Holly Hughes, Ethyl Eichelberger, Moe Angeles, John Zorn, Charles Busch, John Kelly, Split Britches (Lois Weaver and Peggy Shaw), John Jesurun, Jo Andres, Tom Murrin, Beth Lepides, Jeff Weiss, and Jack Smith. There is an article in that same journal issue called *Theatre Reports An Evening in the East Village 30 November 1984.*[4] This article is made up of a series of descriptions of events at spaces in the East Village on that evening. It is written by people who were there, so there are eight writers who cover eight venues: Club Chandalier, Darinka, 8BC, Limbo Lounge, P.S.122, Pyramid Club, The Shuttle, and WOW Café. This issue is amazing and telling because of the way it grapples with the extraordinary possibility and potential of what is happening with these mostly queer artists and the publics they have amassed on that single night. Each writer is moved by the atmosphere; they relish the feeling, the politics, the sophistication, and richness of the work; but none can refrain from pointing out similar shortcomings (which they always admit are strengths or seem intentional) things, like "bad acting," chaotic spaces, self-consciousness, no parameters (shows could run from 15 minutes to 4 hours), and the feeling of little distinction between artists and audiences. What comes across in these reports is a sense that audiences didn't always know what to expect, that one could count on being surprised, and that there was a profound sense of ownership among everyone involved. That there was a shared commitment to the evening's potential and possibility. The artists had a kind of virtuosity that allowed them to move through more than one venue in a night. Both Moe Angelos and Carmelita Tropicana appeared in performances in two different venues on November 30, 1984.

Around this same time, Jeff Weiss was making his serial drama *That's How the Rent Gets Paid.* He started performances at midnight so that Broadway actors could perform after their shows; and those midnight shows would run until 4, 5, or 6 am. Then artists and audience would go out for breakfast. The downtown theater dance and performance scene was carried by a compulsion to be together, to live big.

The roughness and unpolished elements of the performances were often described in the reports as endearing, necessary, and rich - while, at the same time, the writers felt compelled to remind the reader of what was lacking or "unprofessional" or unresolved. Maybe it was just queer.

Permission to Imagine Our Publics

It's important to address audiences, publics, and institutions at the outset because we do not make work in a vacuum. Yet, neither do we make work for everyone. And although this second assertion that "we do not make work for everyone" is necessary to the queer auteur director, it is important for you to know, if you don't already, that this is not something with which a producer would readily agree – given that one of the defining aspects of theater is the captive audience, "How," I can hear the producer asking, "can I expect to fill seats if you don't set out to captivate everyone?"

Typically, an audience gathers by choice. They are not captive because they've been kidnapped, but because the show is built for an audience to stay for the duration of the event. To get up and walk away can be disruptive, but it is not impossible. By showing up and staying for the entire show, the spectator accepts an invitation, a proposal. What has been proposed? Who is making this invitation? Does the spectator offer up anything? What is the implicit agreement?

The audience becomes a public or was already a public or will be a public to something that is happening in that room or to someone like the writer, an actor, or to the subject matter of the material itself. In his essay "Publics and Counterpublics," Michael Warner elaborates on different kinds of publics, pointing to the critical difference between *the* public and *a* public. "*The* public is a kind of social totality. Its most common sense is that of the people in general."[5] The Oxford English Dictionary (OED) defines *the* public as "a collective group regarded as sharing a common cultural, social, or political interest, but who as individuals do not necessarily have any contact with one another."[6] There may be as many publics as polities, but as Warner points out, when "*one* public is addressed as *the* public, the others are assumed not to matter."[7]

By addressing *a* public as opposed to *the* public you are honing in on "the section of society which is interested in or supportive of the person referred to; *esp.* a writer's readership; a performer's audience."[8] Warner differentiates this kind of public not as one that is the possession of anyone or anything, but as one formed by choice – making it *a* public:

A public can also be a second thing: a concrete audience, a crowd witnessing itself in visible space, as with a theatrical public. Such a public also has a sense of totality, bounded by the event or by the shared physical space. A performer onstage knows where her public is, how big it is, where its boundaries are, and what the time of its common existence is.[9]

Like Warner, I want to draw distinction between an audience and a public. Warner uses the adjective "concrete" to mark an audience as the people, or witnesses, in a space.

The generic use of the term audience often enacts a collapse of two terms: audience and spectator. An early definition of **spectator** is "A person who sees, or looks on at, some scene or occurrence; a beholder, onlooker, observer."[10] Early uses of the word audience derive from a political occurrence of attending a legal hearing. The use of audience over time becomes conflated with spectatorship where an audience is "All the people within hearing of something; (hence) the assembled listeners or spectators at a public performance or event (as a play, film, lecture, etc.) considered collectively."[11] But audience can also mean "those people who admire, support, or take a consistent interest in a particular person, area of artistic activity, idea, etc.; (also) those people who are regarded as likely to be interested in such a person or thing."[12] This audience is quite like Warner's notion of a public.

While it's not necessary, or possible, to bar this slippage, it does feel helpful to identify it *as* slippage or intentional co-mingling and to remember the concrete operations that go soft. From spectator, it feels critical to retain its reliance on "seeing" or on what is made visible. With audience, it feels significant that it arises from a body called upon to judge or parse. And with public, I want to remember the constant pressure that *the* public exerts on *a* public. This pressure aligns with the pressures of the state, the institution, the producer, even the dramaturg who conjure *the* public to justify the powers, conventions, and normativities that they uphold.

Your Public, Your Audience, Your Spectator

As an example of an early use of the word spectator, the OED cites Thomas Hobbes 1651 text *Leviathan* (ii. xxxi. 189): "A signe is not a signe to him that giveth it, but to him to whom it is made; that is, to the spectator."[13] Hobbes implies it is the spectator who determines the message or meaning of a work or, at the very least, must accept it or receive it.

Perhaps it is heavy handed to bring Hobbes and his provocative treatise *Leviathan* into this essay. But (*come on!*) let's admit that he did it first, using the imagery of theater to define the political. It's seductive that some of the earliest theorization on social contracts identifies the outsized role spectators play in the making of meaning and the relevance of audience desire or agreement on the impact of a given work's meaning. Queers traffic in desire; it's desire that awakens our queer impulses. Hobbes' sign is activated by a desiring relation between the maker and the spectator. In this sense, an audience is a public because they appear (already) to themselves. Warner further defines a public through seven conditions:

1 A public is self-organized.
2 A public is a relation among strangers.
3 The address of public speech is both personal and impersonal.

4 A public is constituted through mere attention.
5 A public is the social space created by reflexive circulation of discourse.
6 Publics act historically according to the temporality of their circulation.
7 A public is world making.[14]

Queer Publics, Counterpublics, Performance Utopias

The performance scholar Jill Dolan, also once a (queer) director, writes about desire from the vantage point of audience in her book *Utopia in Performance: Finding Hope at the Theater.* Dolan calls up temporary communities and public spheres:

> Utopia in Performance . . . examines the audience as a group of people who have elected to spend an evening or an afternoon not only with a set of performers enacting a certain narrative arc or aesthetic trajectory, but with a group of other people, sometimes familiar, sometimes strange. I see, in this social choice, potential for intersubjectivity not only between performer and spectators but among the audience, as well. Audiences form temporary communities, sites of public discourse that, along with the intense experiences of utopian performatives, can model new investments in and interactions with variously constituted public spheres.[15]

I think it is also important to point out that, in the case of the Dyke Division project *Room for Cream,* it was not only Dykes and Queers and Transfolk who were showing up for the experience, but also artists, theater makers – the very downtown we were emulating. The address was not just a queer one, but it was a call to another possibility of being together – to a theater that is dumb, smart, uncontained, self-conscious, blunt, magical, and weird. This theater had to rely on the conventions of the theater – on conjuring one reality on top of another and picking and choosing what is made visible. Theater, where the set and world of *Room for Cream* was literally set on top of another show's set. Theater, where the audience had to spend their preshow moments sharing with each other what had happened so far, and often digressed into stories of the conditions of the event as opposed to the plot lines. As the show progressed, the rules of the world also took shape. Sappho, MA was clearly a Utopia; everyone was a lesbian, even the men; Vampires had covens on the outskirts of town; and transmen named Oak and Willow ran a goat farm on a squat. Wally Shawn played a medium who spoke with Mary Todd Lincoln and opened a rival business to Room for Cream (the lesbian-owned café and the main setting of the drama) called The Tea Bag (if you don't know that reference, you can look it up). The local prison played Oxygen Network all day long. There were plenty of glory holes in the bathroom stalls. Long lost lovers showed up in the bodies of men; and our little old ladies were wanted, radical activists who had gone underground. There were murders, accidental beheadings, and wild elections where the audience somehow voted a three-way tie for the candidates – with 165 votes each candidate got exactly 55 votes! So the town had three mayors, and they mandated that Sapphoites use the single pronoun "o" for everyone.

The experience of making *Room for Cream* was a kind of fever dream of pleasure. We were able to react in real time to the public that had amassed, and the performers were deeply drawn to the show. The cast grew as we peopled the world with new characters and ever more complicated plotlines. Many in the cast cleared their schedules for months, just so they could be guaranteed consistent plotlines and become regular characters. But there was also intense pressure as the desires of everyone involved compounded. We realized that in our last regular season, we were building toward a few heteronormative plot finales, like a marriage and a baby being born. This was before gay marriage was legal, and there was a lot of conflict in the queer community around this issue. As we moved toward our season finale, a wedding, we were like, "What are we doing? This is a hugely divisive issue." So, we sent an e-mail to our subscriber audience. (At this point, we were in our third season and had to run the show twice in an afternoon to accommodate our audiences. Because our audience had grown frustrated with how quickly tickets sold out the previous season, we also allowed for a subscriber audience who had bought tickets to all episodes in advance of the season.) The email we sent asked them to write to us about their opinions and thoughts on marriage. We didn't want our audience to go un-acknowledged because we understood that they had inserted themselves into the project. We ended up using their words in the script, and the wedding scene devolved into an argument/conversation which then got interrupted by a baby being born, a murder, and some other things. In the end, no one knows whether the wedding concludes. This episode was also packed with queer icons and artists like Jibz Cameron aka Dynasty Handbag, Faye Driscoll, Martha Wilson, DJ Amber Valentine, Randy Harrison from Queer as Folk, Nicky Paraiso singing love songs, and us. It was so satisfying.

But the show was unsustainable. Nobody was paid; we kept tickets prices at $8 and used all the money on set pieces and props for each show and rehearsal rental space. We all were having to say no to other things in our lives; I was driving 3 hours each way for rehearsal twice a week. We had all the support in the world, a frenzy of support, and yet we also had none at all. As the producer, director, and co-writer, as well as an actor in the show, I opted to let it end.

I needed the thought space. I needed to understand what this show was, I needed to come back to the theater in a different way. Throughout *Room for Cream*, I continued working as/with Two-headed Calf as a professional company. After *Room for Cream* ended, we made an opera, *You, my Mother,* with the new music ensemble Yarn/Wire. And I had a baby. And I started a project that was billed as performance-as-research titled *I'm Bleeding All Over the Place: Studies in directing or nine encounters between me and you.*

Reading the Audience

When I began the performance-as-research project, *I'm Bleeding All Over the Place*, my ambition was to study the director's relationship to an audience as it is mediated through all the elements of a performance. In the book is an addendum that documents a handful of notecards, with handwritten real-time responses, collected from three separate audiences of this project. The overriding theme of these audience responses is their self-awareness as participants in the event and their willingness to name their own desires. When I say participants, I do not mean that the audience felt involved in participatory theater, but rather that they recognized their own role as audience in the creation of value. From this recognition, there was a balance between those who owned their experience and those who demanded that the experience meet their (unspoken) needs and desires.

Then there were others whose presence and attention strayed ecstatically and joyfully beyond the concerns of the performance. They wrote things like "Do you want to get hamburgers after this?" and "Do you think Erin will meet us at the bar later?" – using the cards to pass notes and make plans with friends and, therefore, suggesting that perhaps their minds were already on what happens after the show.

What was clear in these cards was that audiences don't always feel permission to own their experience and, as a result, rebel against the work and the theater. This is a problem and also pleasure of the captive audience. Captivity forces an awareness of time, space, and commitment – and perhaps even belonging. *Why have I agreed to this?* These conditions of the theater and the captive audience are almost exotic and for many quite destabilizing.

The first three encounters of *I'm Bleeding All Over the Place* allowed the audience to assume a role of expert or investigator of the event in front of them.

In cards 1 and 2, audience members speculate on how the actors' physical choices make the audience feel. For example, they found one actor's choice of sitting during a scene "very powerful"[16] and wondered about lying down or being in the dark; another spectator wished the actors would push the couch around, speculating on what else *could* happen on stage.

In card 5, the audience member wrote: "Best atmosphere I've ever felt in this space . . . . This atmosphere? I feel like you slipped me a drink."[17] This comment is curious – they are surprised to experience pleasure in occupying the space while also playfully accusing the artist of drugging them. It may be that the same elements that cause revolt and resistance in a performance are the very aspects that cause great pleasure. And this is the rub – the important and specific issue that brings us to the politics of encounters in the theater.

In card 4 an audience member, who I know attended all three events, writes about their second night:

I came back for the second day. I realized upon walking in that I have no expectations. It's as though I wasn't here before. I think you have opened up a transgressive, maybe a real challenging and generous space. So generous! It gives and gives maybe to the point of transgression . . .?[18]

This card is awesome, not because it is supportive of the project, but because of its discordant equivalences. That having no expectations and feeling challenged feels generous and like a gift. And that excessive giving is transgressive. Transgression here seems to give ecstatic pleasure though transgression, by definition, requires forgiving.

A transgression is something that is against a command or law. Whether you are cheating on a test, or cheating on a spouse, you are committing transgressions that are not easily forgiven. A transgression is a failure to do your duty. A sin is a transgression against God.[19]

Transgression is significant to our insistence of being queer auteur directors. You transgress when you undermine the norms or the genre. In my experience, transgressors get punished. Certainly, the transgressive director gets punished by the people upholding the norms and the genre, producers, and presenters. They are punished by having resources withheld.

Yet transgressions, for us and our publics, are vital; they open up new worlds. Just look to one of our most famous transgressors, Colin Kaepernick. Through his transgressive actions, most notably that of taking a knee, he opened new avenues of experience for professional athletes *and* spectators. His actions refused and condemned white supremacy and American hypocrisy, but also the idea that athletes can't use their voice and should not be political. His actions address his public (which extended well beyond the spectators of a football game). The public was already there and ready for his act, and with his act, their power grew. His gesture drew out his public and made them visible enough to influence the landscape of politics in sports.

Who is it that contains us, our publics, and our transgressions?

A Life in the Field

As an artist who has made a career in the downtown theater scene, who has made do with too little, but who has been deeply supported by a community of artists, queers, and scholars, I still CANNOT glory in the freedoms that I gained through working around scarcity. I could thrive because I came to myself in a situation where people said yes, or where I could brush aside nos. But it came at a cost; my survival demanded that I ask my collaborators to also merely survive –which is unsustainable for collaborative practices.

Everybody suffers when radical yeses aren't available to all of us all of the time. There must be a way to stop fantasizing about hole-in-the-wall venues where "everybody knows your name," and to start claiming the stages and lights and paychecks to make rooms where "your people" are welcome. They want "your people," so they need to embrace you. Not as a star but as an artist who makes a life here in this field. If we are to work together in this field, we need to hold each other; we need to be purposeful of what we ask of the field and what it asks of us. We need to hold what it promises and push against what it fails at. We can embrace the burdens and ecstatic delights of the work because we have chosen to live here.

Notes

1 Eve Kosofsky Sedgwick, "Queer and Now," in *Tendencies* (London: Routledge, 1994), 3.
2 About Us (2020, October 20) Retrieved from www.lmda.org. *This description was changed with website updates as of April 2021.
3 Amy Steele, *Dramaturgy 101: Illuminating the World of the Play* (2021, April 3, 2021) Retrieved from www.schooltheatre.org/publications/featurearticles/dramaturgy101.
4 "An Evening in the East Village: 30 November 1984," The Drama Review: TDR 29, no. 1 (1985): 25–56.
5 Michael Warner, "Publics and Counterpublics," in *Public Culture* (Duke University Press, Volume 14, Number 1, Winter, 2002), 49.
6 Public n. (2018). In Oxford Online Dictionary. Retrieved from https://www-oed-com.proxy.library.upenn.edu.
7 Michael Warner, *Publics and Counterpublics* (New York: Zone Books, 2002), 66.
8 Public *n.* (2018). In *Oxford Online Dictionary*. Retrieved from https://www-oed-com.proxy.library.upenn.edu.
9 Michael Warner, *Publics and Counterpublics* (New York: Zone Books, 2002), 66.
10 Spectator *n.* (2018). In *Oxford Online Dictionary*. Retrieved from https://www-oed-com.proxy.library.upenn.edu.
11 Audience *n.* (2018). In *Oxford Online Dictionary*. Retrieved from https://www-oed-com.proxy.library.upenn.edu.

12 Ibid.
13 Spectator *n.* (2018). In *Oxford Online Dictionary*. Retrieved from https://www-oed-com.proxy.library.upenn.edu.
14 Michael Warner, *Publics and Counterpublics* (New York: Zone Books, 2002).
15 Jill Dolan, "Introduction," from Utopia in Performance: Finding Hope at the Theater (University of Michigan Press, 2005), 10.
16 Note cards 1 and 2. See addendum before this chapter.
17 Note card 5. See addendum before this chapter.
18 Note card 4. See addendum before this chapter.
19 Transgression (April 2, 2021). Retrieved from https://www.vocabulary.com/dictionary/transgression.

Essay Three

DEEP LISTENING, OR I CAN'T TELL YOU HOW TO DO THAT PLAY

Grace

I have been preparing to write this book for a long time. I spent several years making the "research-as-performance project" *I'm Bleeding All Over the Place* in order to tease out what lies beneath the director's practice. For a while, I thought I might be writing a textbook. Then I tried my hand at something more akin to critical theory. But with each approach, the ideas got lost in the trappings of the genre I was working in. The thing about me is that for every non-fiction book I read, I probably read 20 novels. It was through my love of novels that I came upon the writer Marilynne Robinson and her book of essays, *The Givenness of Things*. This book unleashed me. The essay was the form. Through the essay Robinson weaves her Christian beliefs, liberal ideology, and extreme common sense with her scholarship to help the reader comprehend this moment (cultural, historical, ideological, political) by asking us to consider the givenness of things, or what is known. I am not Christian, but Robinson unapologetically teaches me to see the world and engage its problems through her Christian lens. This feels akin to asking all my readers to engage what queerness has to offer to their practice.

I invoke Robinson because she demonstrated for me that the essay is a genre or form that gives me permission to embrace my years of experience and accumulation of knowledge as a ground from which to invite you into conversation. I invoke Robinson because she appeals to her readers to seek the potential in all their encounters. She's open, engaged, contemplative, and fun. In her essays, Robinson does not shy away from opening exclamations of awe like, "Existence is remarkable, actually incredible."[1] She's willing to be playful and personal, often commenting on her own statements with dandy little sentences like this one: "All very well."[2] And, more importantly, she implicates us all in her grasping toward the potential of our humanity. She strives to guide her reader to embrace what is given.

One such given is the experience of grace, which she describes like this:

It is meant to suggest the feeling all of us have who try something difficult and find that, for a moment or two perhaps, we succeed beyond our aspirations. The character

DOI: 10.4324/9781003253402-4

on the page speaks in her own voice, goes her own way. The paintbrush takes life in a painter's hand, the violin plays itself. There is no honest answer to the inevitable questions: Where did that idea come from? How did you get that effect? Again, particulars are lacking. We have no language to describe the sense of a second order of reality that comes with these assertions of higher insights and will override even very settled intentions, when we are fortunate.[3]

It strikes me that all of these examples are of creative leaps. Grace, as described here, happens to the artist. Can you relate to this experience that she calls grace? I can. I would even say that I strive for it. Whether or not we agree that grace comes from "higher insights," I would argue that an aptitude for overriding "settled intentions" is something that you can hone. This state that Robinson calls grace does not have to arrive out of nowhere (or from above), it can be invited into our practices.

In this essay, my essay, I propose you engage an openness to form and trust that the voice of the project will arise through a practice of deep listening. I will linger on the dynamic space of the rehearsal room and all of its potential. But I will not tell you how to do that play.

I Will Not Tell You How To Do That Play

In *The Givenness of Things* Robinson writes,

> The most persistent and fruitful traditions of American literature from Emily Dickinson to Wallace Stevens is the meditation on the given, the inexhaustible ordinary. Ralph Waldo Emerson and William James wrote about the subtle and splendid process of consciousness in this continuous encounter.[4]

Robinson's "subtle and splendid process of consciousness in the continuous encounter" describes the way the rehearsal room ought to be approached. I typically call this approach seeing and listening, which could be juxtaposed with prescribing and insisting. I posit that we build a rehearsal room and a process that allows the work to reveal itself; construct a working method that allows our assumptions to be present and to be in conversation rather than in conflict. Deep listening is not about hearing, but about being fully present to what is happening in the encounter with a work in order to gather meaning.

The term Deep Listening, as many of you may know, is a practice coined by the lesbian composer Pauline Oliveros, who engaged listening as a kind of immersive introspective experimentation that allowed her to engage composition as activism and community building. For Oliveros, "Listening is directing attention to what is heard, gathering meaning, interpreting and deciding action."[5]

Here listening translates to a technique for gathering and interpreting. This then allows you to decide on an action.

Given Circumstances

While directing, you'll want to do a similar kind of gathering; you'll identify the conditions that inform your rehearsal room. You'll want to consider practical conditions like how the actors are trained, who the project is for, how much time you have, what kind of script you're working with, what values and systems are used by the institution(s) inviting you to direct, and so on. These conditions could be considered the given circumstances of your project. I am borrowing the term *given circumstances* from Konstanin Stanislavsky and his acting system. In Stanislavsky's System the *given circumstances* detail all of the conditions of the immediate moment that a character must navigate as they work for their *wants*. Stanislavsky suggests that these circumstances not only affect a character's ability to achieve their wants, but these circumstances inform their wants. The actor trained in this system is taught to identify these given circumstances in order to establish and achieve their objective(s). This process, originally introduced as an element of Stanislavsky's system for acting, relies on practical lessons drawn from observations of human behavior. As a director, you can borrow from this discovery and can identify the given circumstances of your project before you make choices about your approach to the rehearsal room. These given circumstances affect and inform how you identify and reach your objectives, how you lead the project, and how you build a practice. They can't be ignored or discarded because they are the conditions of making, they will shape how you work. Recognizing what is given is a kind of listening that helps you to develop a process.

Directing Is a Practice

I cannot tell you how to do that play because directing is a practice and not a craft. This distinction matters because the difference between a practice and a craft is the difference that allows for the "subtle and splendid process of consciousness in the continuous encounter."

When I hear that someone is a good craftsperson, I imagine a kind of perfection or tidiness. Craft relies on deep skills and honed experience with the tools of the craft. The quality of the work is recognizably good. To become a good craftsperson requires following a process through which you improve your skills, through intensive study, and through repetition and attention to fine details. Theater relies on craft for the training of actors and designers (and sometimes playwrights). Much of the craft of the American theater has origins in the extensive study that was the life work of Stanislavsky. Many great artists and thinkers have continued his work by building new approaches to craft. As an acting teacher, I love teaching and thinking about these methods. I relish the depth of choice and the range of knowledge that these highly developed, honed skills instill in trained actors and how they inform designers. *All very well.* However, knowing craft and executing knowledge with skill is not the same as being present to the things happening in the room or tracing an impulse. It is not the same as developing a process that allows the work to open up to you; it is not the same as having a practice.

Practice is different from craft because a practice builds on an additional kind of knowledge; I might even say a passion. To build a practice, you engage the craft, the study, the history of theater – even with distance and some doubt, with ambivalence or a differing perspective. You don't assume that merely honing and reproducing skills makes the work meaningful. A practice creates space for you to engage craft and utilize it, but it also asks that you absorb what is useful and discard components that lead you astray or block your own understanding of the thing you are making. A practice allows for the possibility that *good* is ambiguous. Practices not only allow for the director to articulate their point of view, but they depend on a continual interrogation of one's own skills, investments, and relationships to collaborators and to audience. Practices also allow for difference and refusal – and, potentially, for moments of grace.

Building a working process is a means of addressing or even growing a practice. But what can a practice look like?

Let's consider the auteur. I'll remind you that auteur is a term that is derived from film theory and describes a kind of director that uses the camera as a pen. In film, *auteur theory* argues that the director uses the visual and technical elements of the film, rather than plotline to convey the message.[6]

Like film auteurs, theater auteurs rely on process and form as a kind of authoring (the pen). Theater auteurs have built practices that rely on the use of rehearsal vocabularies and processes that they develop over the course of the project or their career. These directors invite a kind of exploration and discovery phase into the rehearsal room. A process doesn't necessarily have to be repeatable, but should be developed with the intention of engaging the whole collaborative team in shared questions or explorations – toward an end goal – however open that is.

My insistence on practice is not a refusal of the reliance that theater has on craft; it is a refusal to rely on good craft translating into meaningful experiences in the theater. Some experts (i.e., educators, artistic directors, granting organizations) will imply that those who know craft make good work; they even use this idea to silence unique voices and to resist change. The richness of the American theater was built on the work of great auteur directors and experimental writers (artists who developed unique practices despite being taught a craft or despite feeling alienated from the theater). Still, there is too little permission to break from the tradition of craft and imagine radical new approaches to the rehearsal room.

Process

Building a practice means giving yourself permission to move toward your impulses and vision. To make any sense of this, we should parse out what takes place in rehearsal. How does a show get made? I'll start with the caveat that everything I am about to say happens when making a show could just as often not happen. Don't overthink this breakdown.

One way to describe the steps involved in directing a play:

- A play is chosen or a project conceived of.
- The creative team is pulled together, often including a writer (or script), director, designers, and a producer.
- There is a period of research, of conversation, of imagining the process, and even the end product.
- Performers are brought in. (Again, this order of events can vary depending on the conditions of the collaboration.)
- Rehearsals begin.
- During the rehearsal process, the performers build the show with the creative team. They learn their roles; they build relation; they discover and then set where to go in space and what they are doing in time. They inhabit their roles, they tell stories, they make something happen. This work begins in various ways: sometimes with table work (sitting around a table discussing and analyzing the text and roles) or, other times, with improvisation (exploring the roles and story with open, often non-scripted, exploration of the themes and people). Or you can start with staging or physically

scoring the play (this is less frequently done, but involves blocking) and performing a show before doing the deep analytical work (Kabuki and Noh are examples of this).

- Rehearsal periods can vary wildly as does this process. But the key point here is that a process is necessary, that a process allows growth, change, and the gathering together of the work.
- Closer to the opening date, the show will move into the performance venue, a period during which various components such as lighting, set, sound, costumes, video, etc., are fully integrated. This period is also about establishing more concretely the relationship of the audience to the show and the performers. Where is the audience? What is its proximity to the show? What does that public see – how are they guided or invited into to the story the performers bring? This process involves planning, preparation, and advance thinking work. It also requires days or weeks of implementation and realization. This part of process is called *tech* (short for technical rehearsals).
- Sometimes there are previews – designed to allow for the show to change while playing in front of an audience.
- Then the show happens.
- The show has a life of some distinct duration, and then the show comes down.
- Afterward, it lives on in people's imaginations.
- Or it doesn't.

What should be evident here is the significance of process. Process allows for the creators/collaborator team (including performers) to come together and parse through all the possibilities and to listen to one another and the text (or the playwright). The director guides and holds the process. (In some scenarios, the producer has a heavy hand in this – and the process is formulated well in advance, done the same way every time with less input from the creative team.)

Envisioning and establishing process is where the work of the director is most relevant. Process and relationships are the heart of auteur's practice.

Coaches, Auteurs, and Play Practice

A friend of mine once misremembered our acting teacher and director from college as having worn a whistle around his neck. Like a coach. He didn't.

But it is not so off base to slot your acting teacher or your first director in the same memory bank as your high school coach. Coaches are strategists, but they also support the team in building and sharing common languages; and, when possible, they work to make you better by helping you build on your skills and address your weaknesses. Mostly, they see the big picture, and they make real-time decisions about how your combination of instinct and skills might combine to have the best impact on a field or court. Coaches have game plans, and they have plays. But a winning coach adjusts to new situations and to surprises and teaches their players to do the same. Losing coaches typically have a limited ability to see what is possible. They do not make smart real-time adjustments because they are locked into decisions or assumptions made a while back.

Theater is not a sporting event. But I worry that the way we teach or think about directing reinforces decisions or assumptions that were, in fact, made a while back – a game plan for another time, another text, and another set of players. The pedagogy of the theater banks on systems, craft, and truisms.

It becomes a scene about a grape on the floor (or the lessons inside the lessons)

"It becomes a scene about a grape on the floor" is an expression I have encountered multiple times in my theater education, I guess as a way of addressing the importance of what is seen. The idea is that, if an actor unintentionally drops a grape on the floor and ignores it for the rest of the scene, the audience will become fixated on the grape on the floor. The grape is what they will see.

In graduate school I was given additional *grape on the floor* guidance; this instruction was labeled *bring in the kites*.

Bring in the kites is a story my grad directing professor told about a time when he was assisting on a summer-stock play. Typically, summer-stock plays (often Lorte productions) are cast long before the summer season. The actors who commit to these roles are asked to learn the script in advance of arriving at the theater, which is usually outside of the city in a town where people "summer." The cast arrives off-book (*script memorized*) for a brief rehearsal and tech period, and then the play goes up. This is often a perfunctory exercise in staging a play: professional theater performed for vacationers. It so happened that the summer of the *kites* production (which, if my memory serves, was a production of *Breakfast at Tiffany's*), one of the actors quit the show the day the performers were scheduled to leave NYC for the theater in upstate NY. The director and his assistant (my professor) stopped by the Equity Actors Guild offices on their way out of town to file a complaint. While in the Equity office, they met an actor sitting in the lobby, who was willing to replace the actor who quit – who would, in fact, join them on their trip upstate. They hired this new actor and spent the drive upstate drilling him on his lines. This newly hired actor, it turned out, was bad at this role. When the play was set to open, the director "solved" the bad actor problem by distracting the audience every time the actor was on the stage. The theater happened to be an old barn with barn doors behind the stage. The director asked the designer to place kites all about on the stage; and each time the actor came on stage, the stage crew opened the barn doors and the kites flittered and floated about in the wind. As a result, the story goes, the audience had no recollection of ever having seen the actor on the stage because they were watching the kites.

For years, the lessons I took from the *grape on the floor* and *bring in the kites* is that audiences are easily distracted or that you can lose their attention to all kinds of possible attention-grabbing elements. The *grape on the floor* is an example of an unwanted consequence of an actor's bad decision. Here you have actors so focused on what they had rehearsed and what they are doing that they cannot adjust to a little mistake. They drop a grape, but they have not rehearsed dropping the grape, so they go about the scene as if the grape never dropped. But the audience is thinking, "pick up that grape!" Throughout the rest of the performance, the audience will continue to watch, and maybe even worry about, the grape. Maybe the grape will roll somewhere else on stage. Maybe the grape will get stepped on. *Bring in the kites* is offered as an example of a presumably good decision by a director to cover for a bad actor. Here the easily distracted audience supports the production for the very reason that their attention wanders away from that which the director does not want seen – the bad actor.

But how do these lessons translate to the rehearsal room? What does it mean in regards to the process of making a show? I admit that, as a teacher, I parroted the grape lesson to my own students. But over the years I grew frustrated, perplexed, and then ultimately excited about the whimsy of the audience. Why would they sit around thinking about a grape while something is happening on stage? Is that really what's happening to our audiences? Do we even know what is happening to our audiences? How do we attend to that relationship? Do we want to teach actors to pick up their grapes? How do we make the grape do something to our audience, or better yet how do we help the actor do things to our audience?

Deep Listening/Seeing

To me, the lesson points to the question I posited before: *what are we seeing*? Meaning also, how is what we are doing translating to an audience? What is everyone looking at? And what is the disparity between what we look at and what we see? We may all be looking at the same thing, but we are certainly not all seeing the same thing. Can we engage our audience in a kind of deep seeing? Do we do this through how we engage the text itself and each other in the rehearsal room?

Here I am intentionally using seeing and listening interchangeably, similar to how the word audience (audio) and spectator (sight) are used interchangeably.

To return to Pauline Oliveros, Oliveros differentiates listening from hearing by saying that "listening is to give attention to what is perceived"[7] and that "When listening there is a constant interplay with the perception of the moment compared with remembered experience – listening is subject to time delays."[8] Oliveros' experiments in deep listening can influence our work to build a practice that allows for awareness of a shared and divergent experience. Oliveros addressed the shared experience of live performance, knowing that each audience member experiences the event singularly while also in common-ness or in community. This creates time-delays that affect listening – which brings me back to Warner's ideas of both the historical temporality of circulation of discourse and the reflexive circulation of discourse. We are listening and we are seeing, but always simultaneously we are drawing that experience into discourse with all the experiences that moment collides with. I believe that the event of the performance creates a pulse among the participants and that happens in the room as we are experiencing the same thing differently. Our breath, our focus (or lack of), our gasps, our laughs, and everything present create a space that activates deep seeing. Actors know what this feeling is because much of actor training is designed to enable a kind of *immediate* awareness of each other and the space. What I mean by immediate here is that we are holding open an awareness to the others on the stage and their words (even when we have heard the words many times before). But the performers are not the only people who can be immediate in the theater.

In the published translation of the Japanese Noh actor Zeami's treatises on Noh acting, Zeami (1363–1443) repeatedly considers ideas of awareness, within the actor, in relation to the elements on stage and in relation to the audience. In the treatise titled Mirror Held to the Flower, Zeami writes about Matching the Feeling to the Moment. He begins this argument by addressing the connection between the performer and the audience:

In the performance of *sarugaku*, when the actor first appears there is one particular instant when the opening speech should properly begin. It must not be too soon. Nor must it be too late. First the actor leaves the green room [sic], stops as he approaches the stage from the bridge, takes cognizance of the audience, and then just when the spectators think he is to begin his opening speech, he must commence at exactly that instant when his feelings match those of his audience.[9]

I am often inspired by this treatise from the Japanese medieval period because of Zeami's constant consideration of the energies that flow in the space of performance. He emphasizes the many points of tension and shared awareness, thus the mirror held to the flower. He also discusses relationships between listening and seeing.

This immediacy is a kind of pulse, or liveness in the process, that the director can draw out. And this is possible through agreeing to listen or see what is happening in each moment as something perceived. This, of course, is complicated by the idea that perception is subject to time delays. This too produces a pulse that we must stay in – or remain active in.

Oliveros is not only addressing listening, she is addressing deep listening. According to her, "Deep has to do with complexity, boundaries or edges beyond the ordinary or habitual understandings."[10] She explains that "A deep thinker defies stereotypical knowing, learning to expand the perception of sounds into the whole space time continuum, connected to the whole of the environment and beyond."[11] She invites us to "notice what you are hearing and expand your listening to continually include more."[12] I would call this a practice.

What Happens at Play Practice

Anecdote – When I was in graduate school for directing, I was telling my directing professor about my plans for play practice that week. He was horrified, livid. I was never to call rehearsal "play practice" ever again, he demanded – at least not in his presence anyhow. Now, I start every rehearsal process by asking everyone in the room if we can agree to call what we are doing *play practice*.

I do this to claim my own relationship to the rules, but also to gather force against the correctness of craft. Time spent in play practice is the time to discover, to experiment, to find the possibility of the work, and to build in magical properties and co-reliances.[13] (See appendix image of Karinne Keithley Syers "Queer Poetics" Comix).

I wish such play practices for you, too.

You can use deep seeing as a mode of working. Deep seeing allows you to step back from making prescriptive choices; it asks that you hold impulses at bay and that you resist forcing something to mean something right away. You can make space for witnessing, without judgment or conclusion. This isn't easy because people in a rehearsal room are often intent on sticking to decisions – they have been trained to analyze texts and make decisive determinations about character and objectives based on a myriad of actor training systems and methods.

Most actors will make strong choices; they will draw out the conflict and show their character. This is all productive in rehearsal because this teaches you how they see, or what they need. Excess can be interesting. It's all interesting and possible, so find a way to hang back and let the room be a little messy. Take your time. Find, in the mess, your strategies, your process. Each text, each show, each set of given circumstances demands its own process.

This process work might rely on good instincts, on an understanding of what needs focus and when, on time management, on knowing when to push and work something, and knowing when you can let it be because the actor will find their way on their own or that the moment has not revealed itself yet.

I like a process that allows the work to reveal itself. This is why listening and seeing is so impactful on my process. This is why I choose not to pre-determine what the play *is*. Often times when I am watching a play, it's obvious to me that the director had an end goal in mind and worked throughout the rehearsal period to squeeze that vision out of the play – out of the actors – and out of the design. What you get at the end of the show is a kind of wash (or haze) of a concept or story; the risk is that you leave your audience (and perhaps your collaborators) feeling outside of the experience.

Making space for a play to reveal itself is different from being indecisive or meandering through a lot of choices and hoping for a discovery. It does not foreclose the importance of rigor. Your time is limited, and your collaborators' time is valuable. You can set up the conditions in the room so work can be rigorous. So much has to get done at play practice: the actors have to navigate the physical space, they need to speak their lines, they need to hear one another, they need to feel the script, and they need to be in their bodies together. Keeping actors actively engaging in the text gives them so much opportunity to listen to and inhabit the world, to imagine possibilities, and take action. Some directors spend an inordinate amount of time talking about what they are doing – how they are feeling, why the work is important – this can be so deadly. This approach lulls everyone in the room into believing that having thoughts and impressions about the work is the same as materializing the work. It resists coming to discovery inside and through practice.

Something Planned and Something Unplanned

What does this have to do with the grape or the kites? An actor who is deep seeing will also see the grape. An audience who sees and considers the grape is expanding their understanding of the event in front them. Actors study improvisation in order to cope with these misplaced grape problems. But also, the original point of the grape lesson is to warn actors, to point out that they must be aware of everything around them. That they must absorb and respond to the moment that is happening. That, inside of the repeated actions and words they perform each evening, they must also be immediate and aware and responsive. Ah – I love the puzzle of this task – the build-up of memories in a live setting – the sameness that is never the same.

But what about the kites? I actually find this story mean-spirited and lazy. I was told about the kites as a lesson in how to successfully solve a problem of "bad acting." It's a smoke and mirrors solution. I do like that it uses something we know about focus to make something else happen, that it points to some sense of understanding of the room or understanding of what we may be seeing. But what does drawing the audience's attention to kites do to the event of the play? It would appear that every time that actor walked on the stage, everything is lost. The actor. The text. The other people. The plot.

Also, what does it mean that the director wants to disappear a so-called bad actor? And what does it mean that he was bad actor? Could it be possible that the director was a bad director? I would prefer to drop the word bad altogether, along with all of the sloppy critique that is bound up with it. Instead, we can pinpoint what is causing the cringe feeling that sets off the "bad" alarm. There is typically a kind of disconnect happening somewhere. And this is what you as a director can make space to see. Deep seeing can allow you to break down what is happening in these moments of "bad acting," and it can help you to find new ways to address the actor. Forget that the actor is "bad"; it's just not true. The actor, in all their complexity, is there in the moment with you; and that is your reality. Maybe you can switch their tasks or focus on something more physical. Maybe you can set up a kind of game to play with their lines. I think there is, more often than not, a solution to these problems that does not involve alienation, but that relies on making use of the very instincts that appear, at first glance, to be betraying the actor.

What is most interesting in the anecdotes I learned is that something planned and something unplanned happened when the actor quit and the grape fell. The new actor is replaced by kites, a planned event, and an abandonment of the actor. The grape on the floor is an accident and is unplanned. Both events, dynamically, implicate the audience as a kind of author.

What these stories remind me is that theater as a live event is unpredictable and includes the space of the accident. The audience is also unpredictable, and our assumptions of what is happening with and for our audience are foundationally unstable. And, to be honest, I find this awesome. It's awesome because it demands a complex and fluid response to the conditions; it demands awareness. It asks that we listen deeply. And perhaps it is our actions in response to this intentional practice of gathering and interpreting the given that can allow for moments of grace in our work.

Notes

1 Marilynne Robinson, "Son of Adam, Son of Man," in *The Givenness of Things* (New York: Picador, 2016), 240.
2 Marilynne Robinson, "Realism," in *The Givenness of Things* (New York: Picador, 2016), 273.
3 Ibid., 273–274.
4 Marilynne Robinson, "Reformation," in *The Givenness of Things* (New York: Picador, 2016), 24.
5 Kerry O'Brien, "Listening as Activism: "The Sonic Meditations" of Pauline Oliveros," *The New Yorker* (December 9, 2016).
6 Auteur Theory n. (2022) in *Britannica Online Encyclopedia*. Retrieved from https://www.britannica.com/art/auteur-theory.
7 Pauline Oliveros, "The Difference Between Hearing and Listening," *TEDx Talks* (YouTube, November 12, 2015).
8 Ibid.
9 Zeami translated by J. Thomas Rimer and Yamazaki Masakazu, "Mirror Held to the Flower," in *On the Art of the Nō Drama* (Princeton, NJ: Princeton University Press, 1984), 82.
10 Pauline Oliveros, "The Difference Between Hearing and Listening," *TEDx Talks* (YouTube, November 12, 2015).
11 Ibid.
12 Ibid.
13 Karinne Keithley Syers, "Queer Poetics" from Superheroes of Narrative Comix, https://pelagic-school.net.

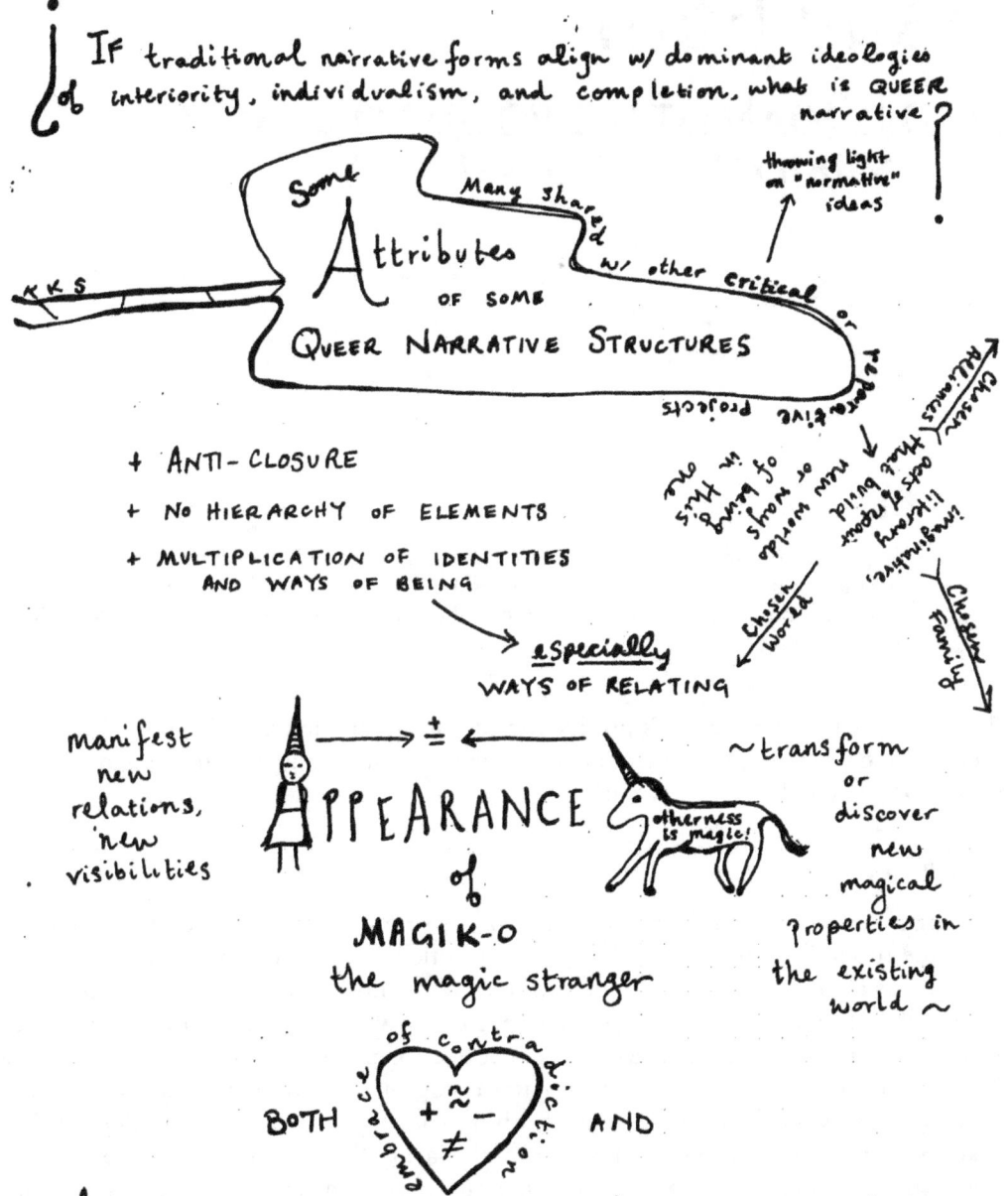

FIGURE 3.1   Karinne Keithley Syers, "Queer Poetics" from Superheroes of Narrative Comix, https://pelagicschool.net.

Essay Four

WHO IS JOAN LITTLEWOOD? OR THE IMPOSSIBILITY OF THE AUTEUR

> Improvisation, immediacy, a jackdaw use of anything and everything to communicate, to bring to life, plays played with, objects juggled, texts exploded, bodies singing, ideas dancing, and all communicating, binding the audience together into the single body of the community.[1]

This describes Joan Littlewood's productions according to Simon McBurney (the auteur director, actor, playwright and founder of England's stunning theater company Complicité). But who is Joan Littlewood?

In the Room

One might know a person by spending time in the room with them. I like to imagine being in the room with the auteur director Joan Littlewood. I like to imagine a rehearsal process that incorporates actor training where we might be learning new ways to relate physically and to alter the energy of a space. Maybe we are marching around in circles copying military gestures and making them comic (or perverse) ala *Oh What a Lovely War* 1963, or building a collapsed mine shaft on stage in order to perform an emotionally explosive scene while squeezed together with nowhere to move (*The Long Shift*, 1951). I like to imagine everyone sitting together and sharing their research. I like to imagine ideas flying around and improvisations being built, even when we have a script in hand. I like to imagine the pleasure in the work and the trust that something would grow out of long days and hours spent together and that the room was a space where the stakes were so high – the pleasure and pain were all knotted-up together. I imagine a room filled with gratitude.

And what about the audience? Can I imagine them? Not who they were specifically, but who they might be? What did they expect or experience from these shows made with such fervor, exhilaration, and mastery? Did they feel the full force of these projects? Did they laugh one moment, perhaps join in on a song – only to remember some brutality of their daily lives in the next moment? Were they empowered? Did they feel seen and feel

DOI: 10.4324/9781003253402-5

heard? Did they perhaps leave the theater feeling a little more like, yes, I am alive and I am here and, despite the odds being stacked against me, I love myself and my neighbor and I will stand with them?

I have had moments in the theater where I was shocked by my experience – moved, excited, and astonished. In these moments you feel the liveness, like something is happening and all of the people there are breathing, feeling, and thinking together. You might feel that life is filled with potential and we are witnessing one another. Being in the room with Joan Littlewood and her work, either as a collaborator or an audience member, must have been an ecstatic experience. She did not waste your time; she grabbed a hold of you and took you on a journey.

Have You Heard of Joan Littlewood?

Even as I conjure us into these rooms with Littlewood, I don't assume that you know who I am talking about. I didn't know who Joan Littlewood was for the first 20 years of my career as a director. So, whether you know of Joan Littlewood or not, could you do me this little favor? Ask the next ten theater professionals you meet, "Who is Joan Littlewood?"

I bet that few of them know of her; or if they have heard of her, they can't really tell you what she did or why she was important. Which is unfortunate. We make work in the wake of many great directors. All the same, directors are vulnerable to obscurity.

One of the greatest and most radical visionaries of the last century, and one of the least studied in U.S. theater institutions, is Joan Littlewood. Yet, Littlewood has become, for me, one of the brightest stars in the constellation of auteurs who guide my path. Joan may not approve of that metaphor. When a young Michael Caine quit her company, the Theatre Workshop, she told him to piss off and then dealt him the insult, "You will only ever be a star."[2]

Rabbit Hole

I learned about Joan Littlewood the same way I discover most things these days – by assigning her on my syllabus. I enjoy teaching because I am greedy to learn, and learning is especially satisfying when experienced through the discoveries my students make. I am selfish when creating challenges for my students, when dishing out the stuff (material) in which they're required to take deep dives, because, like my students, I don't want to be bored. My curiosity about the auteur director became more focused and personal only after I started assigning my directing students to make presentations on *significant* directors. I assigned them directors like Brecht, Grotowski, Suzuki, Bogart, Meyerhold, LeCompte, and Mnouchkine – directors who have had an impact on the field. The assignment was not to give a timeline or biography of the director, but to teach the class about the director's process, their methods, their rehearsal room, and their impact on the field. (Of course, this often does relate to their origin stories.) The aim was to break down and articulate clearly the director's unique practice and how their work continues to influence the field.

In class, I introduce the director project through example. I do the first presentation on Stanislavsky (*that old dog!*) because I am forever awed by his contributions to the theater, his investment in study and systems, and his account of the relationship between the director and actor. I am also inspired by his ability to build terminology, but also by his instinct to continue the work even when it conflicted with or contradicted his own theories. His openness and generosity toward the young experimental directors Vsevolod Meyerhold and Yevgeny Vakhtangov was staggering. Because so much of what we know about theater is grounded in his system, we assume we know the extent of his contributions. But do you really know the depth and breadth of Stanislavsky's influence? Or the influence of so many others before you?

After assigning this project for a few years, I grew bored of hearing about the same handful of directors. I also wanted to expand the assignment to include more women and BIPOC directors. And because Joan Littlewood (whose career spanned from 1935 to 1975) appeared in anthologies on directors and was supposedly known as a "pioneer of the creative ensemble, devised performance, improvisation and for a theater that moved beyond a polite regurgitation of middle-class life to capture the exuberance, wit, and poetry of working-class lives and communities."[3] Equally significant, because in most photographs she looks like a spritely dyke, I pulled her onto the syllabus

Fortunately, an ambitious student agreed to present on Joan. The presentation caught me off guard – not because it was thorough and illuminating (*which it was!*), but because of Joan, because of her work and her legacy. The student herself was enthralled and couldn't contain her awe in discovering Joan Littlewood; the presentation affectively made a deep impression on the class. The specter of Joan hung around that semester, helping to build a collective curiosity and belief in the potential of a director's vision altering the theater. But the question that lingered the most with me was, how was it possible that 20 years into my directing career and over a decade into my teaching career had I never encountered Joan Littlewood? And I can't help but imagine that somehow, somewhere, a little bit of Joan carried through to me.

This is the origin of my own Joan Littlewood rabbit hole.

Why Joan Littlewood Is Important To Me

I was trying to describe this book project to my brother once, and he told me that I should include a chapter titled *Why directing is important to me* – which I immediately dismissed as the stupidest idea. Sometimes when I sit here writing, I think that my brother might be right and that the whole project could exist under the title: *Why directing is important to ME!* For your patient indulgence of these matters of personal importance dear reader, here I can offer you something concrete: *Why Joan Littlewood is important to me.* I am sharing this here because I think Joan Littlewood could become important to you.

There is a lot of information available on Joan's work, life, and career, including a couple great books about her practice written by Nadine Holdsworth. Littlewood wrote her own autobiography, and there is also a detailed and fairly intimate biography of her by Peter Rankin. Follow this trail for yourself. I won't re-do this excellent scholarship but want to pull Littlewood into our conversation here to make an assertion, perhaps heretical!, that Joan is a queer auteur.

Like many artists whose practices were aggressively innovative, she is frequently described as "ahead of her time." To me, being ahead of your time implies being highly attuned to what is possible in your field and being capable of achieving it. Joan learned directing by doing the work and by reading about innovators working across Europe and the Soviet Union and by attempting to translate that work into her process. Littlewood was invested in actor training as part of the rehearsal process at a time when that was unusual for directors. Littlewood was one of the first directors in England to read Stanislavsky's *An Actor Prepares* and incorporate it into her training. She was already attempting to use his system in the 1940s. Littlewood also insisted that everyone involved in making a show with her engage in in-depth study of the material and themes. The entire company served as dramaturgs during the rehearsal practice. She was also technically innovative; she was the first director to use projection design in her shows. She also built huge soundscapes for her plays and convinced a sound designer to build a sound system made of half a dozen turntables that they dragged around Europe to festivals. She brought technical elements into her shows during the rehearsal process, asking that the designers be in the room with them, adding elements as they conceived of them. There was no need for tech rehearsals because the tech was there during the process. This is all very radical considering the conditions in which she was making work.

Joan was born into a working-class family and was raised in poverty. This matters because Peter Brook, who appeared on the theater scene shortly after her, and who also used improvisation and ensemble work, came from great wealth. While Peter Brook was being celebrated as a darling of the English Theater, Littlewood was being harassed, arrested, denied funds, and blacklisted. And yet, if you take a deep dive, you will find that Littlewood was the director that introduced the ensemble company, improvisational rehearsal practices, company-based dramaturgy, complex technical sound and projection design, and Stanislavsky's System of acting to the English Theater. But Brook is often credited for bringing these innovative practices to the English stage.

Joan Littlewood was drawn to the theater as a teenager after having seen a production of Macbeth; she determined that she could do better. At 17 she earned a full scholarship to England's most established theater conservatory, RADA (The Royal Academy of Dramatic Arts), only to withdraw because she didn't like how theater was taught and specifically resented the patrician RADA accents. As a communist who spent much of her early career making agit prop theater with her first company, Theatre of Action, she endured poverty, occasional arrest, and blacklisting while also taking (sometimes under an alias) piecemeal jobs with the national news service BBC to support her ensemble. Joan's ability to create personal interest pieces in local communities made her a favorite among the producers at the BBC, who continued to employ her in secret while she was blacklisted for communism. At the heart of her motivation was a fierce devotion to the working class and their struggles. It was her desire to reach local underserved audiences, and her commitment to her ensemble drove her ambition. She was constantly reimagining the art of the theater, the work of the actor and text, and their relationship to audience – she was not motivated by a dedication to the field of theater but by a drive to reach people through the theater. Ewen McColl, her collaborator and co-founder of her first two companies, Theatre of Action and Theatre Union, described their work as "popular," which we might call "populist." According to McColl, "It wasn't a matter of having less art and more politics but of having more clearly stated politics and more powerful art."[4]

The company often worked in impoverished and desperate conditions. Despite this, Littlewood essentially ran a sophisticated acting studio. She used clear and dedicated training processes that could be considered decadent for the time: she did things like incorporating the physical training of the visionary choreographer Rudolph Laban into rehearsals, designing a training regimen for the purpose of recognizing and extending the actor's vocal range, and using improvisation to build an ensemble company. She worked to build up the performers' strengths to amplify one another; she refused to foreground a star who would diminish the others.

It was because of Joan's lifelong dedication to making shows for the working class and the non-theater-going public that she could lure incredible humans into her companies – people whom she trained to become great actors, writers, and designers. Together they created shows that ultimately would transform theater. Despite her commitment to making work on the periphery in church basements, dancehalls, and clubs, Joan became known throughout much of Europe as one of England's most exciting and innovative directors. Her company, the Theater Workshop, was awarded spots in major European festivals, an honor that the establishment English theater companies were denied. Joan's success on the international stage shocked and infuriated London's theater elite; by contrast these darlings of the English theater chose to reject (and harass) her for much of her early career.

Joan sought to distance herself from the establishment and its audiences; but her work was effective, phenomenal, powerful, and significant; and she couldn't remain on the margins of the field. Also, as her success grew, so did her need for resources. She began to collaborate with designers and actors who crossed over with the West End. In the end, her plays, *Oh What a Lovely War*, *The Quare Fellow*, *The Hostage*, and *A Taste of Honey*, made a profound impact on the English theater and on Broadway in the US.

Joan's relentless dedication to her work raised the stakes of everything she made – the work had to be meaningful. Always buckling down, always finding a path, always demanding the most of herself and her company, she surfaced from obscurity as a force in the field. Despite the fact that very few of your theater friends know of her (*I'm not sure if you have gotten around to asking them, but don't forget to do that!*), Littlewood is considered "the mother of modern theater."[5]

A life of overcoming resistance and rejection allowed her to build a process, priorities, and language of her own. It also made her a national treasure and a Dame, but it didn't make her content. The West End had little allure for her. After a series of West End hits and transfers to Broadway, she did manage to write and direct the critically acclaimed musical *Oh What a Lovely War* which showcased the depth of her genius and richness of her practice. The musical was a playful and spectacular gut punch: it exposed the underbelly of a polite society which celebrates the heroics of the young men it sends off to suffer and die. People claim this work as her best. (Although according to Littlewood, "My best stuff nobody saw."[6]) However, once she became an establishment director, making work destined for transfer to the West End, Joan felt done in by the industry. And instead of striving for that version of success, she left her creative home at the Theatre Royal because according to Joan, "when you have to live by exporting bowdlerized versions of your shows as light entertainments for sophisticated West End audiences you're through."[7]

Littlewood then turned away from directing and to other means of bringing art, education, and theater to the working class. She attempted to use her success to realize her life-long dream of a People's Palace which she called the Fun Palace. She designed plans for the Fun Palace with architect Cedric Price. "Described as both 'a university of the streets' and 'a laboratory of pleasure,' Littlewood envisaged the Fun Palace as a multi-use space housing a series of short-term, frequently updated activities dedicated to pleasure, entertainment, communication and learning."[8]

Littlewood worked tirelessly on the project and assembled a prestigious board of trustees including Buckminster Fuller. She generated funds by agreeing to direct TV commercials and films. In the end, the project was never realized. Realizing the Fun Palace required a leap of faith that people were not ready to make because the project was, again, way ahead of the times.

If you, too, took the time to go down a Joan Littlewood rabbit hole. You may wonder why her achievements aren't more widely celebrated or even taught. From what I can tell, she remains fairly obscure and unknown to American theater directors. This failure is curious.

There is an interview with the Littlewood scholar Nadine Holdsworth in *Essential Drama* where Holdsworth finds herself making this very point:

NH: [Littlewood] completely defied what women and femininity and women in theatre were at that time. So, her as a figure. . . [sic] It was also about her representation of class that really got me interested. She was one of the first figures I came across who presented that authentic working-class voice in a way that wasn't taking the piss, that wasn't belittling those figures in relation to the more dominant socially elevated characters. She was taking them seriously and honoring their experiences. You get it in Oh What a Lovely War with the soldiers in the trenches. Or that experience of those two women in A Taste of Honey, living on the margins of life. They're not seen as dumb or stupid, they're taken seriously and their lives are taken seriously and represented seriously. And the sheer theatrical vibrancy of the work. It is very easy to forget how radical and ground-breaking that was at that time.

PC: You say it is easy to forget...

NH: It has been forgotten.

PC: It is criminal really.[9]

The Quare Fellow

In October 2014, a statue of Joan Littlewood was unveiled at Theatre Royal in Stratford, East London. I've only seen it in pictures, but I love this statue of Joan Littlewood. I like to call it the *quare* fellow, which is the title of the Brendan Behan play that Joan directed with great wit, pizzazz, and empathy. It was through Joan's incredible work with his texts that Behan became famous. And quare is an Irish pronunciation of the word queer (Figure 4.1).

I draw on Joan Littlewood as my prime example of the queer auteur, but you could argue that this quare fellow here isn't queer at all. Her two most significant relationships were with men who were also longtime collaborators. However, there are also narratives of Littlewood having an intimate relationship with a lesbian art teacher. But, for me, Littlewood is queer like theorist Eve Sedgewick is queer. Despite being named a Dame (*note – a dear friend would like me to point out that being named a dame is also **super gay***), Littlewood was the ultimate underdog who worked tirelessly to reflect society from the perspective of those marginalized by power and the establishment. In nurturing and directing Shelagh Delaney's *A Taste of Honey*, Joan risked hostility by staging both a biracial couple and a gay character in pivotal roles in the English theater.

Littlewood is associated with the success of Shelagh Delaney and Brendan Behan whose talents she nurtured. I would argue it was because of Littlewood's ability to hear

FIGURE 4.1   Statue of Joan Littlewood at Theatre Royal Stratford East.

their voices and recognize their humanity and through her incredible talent to translate their works for audiences, that they had the success they did. In the late 1950s, when these plays were staged, a large portion of theater funding in London came through the Arts Council. I don't think they would have given support for Delaney's play if it weren't for Joan's reputation as a "miracle worker" who "was capable of conjuring exciting theater from minimal resources" and for taking under-baked scripts and improvising with them and making judicious edits.[10] When the company applied for money to fund their production of Delaney's *A Taste of Honey* from the Arts Council, their request was approved with this feedback:

1   This is a good bad play. It seems to have been dashed off in pencil in a school exercise book by a youngster who knows practically nothing about the theatre and rather more about life than she can at present digest. There is no self-conscious defiance of established technique . . . Miss Delaney writes with the confidence of sheer ignorance. . .
2   . . . not a play of quality but unnecessarily crude and coarse. If it is the author's intention to shock, she has succeeded. None of the characters ring true and quite often they are completely inconsistent.[11]

Shelagh Delaney was then granted 150 pounds because it has a "sort of strength in its crudity." Littlewood and the Theatre Workshop were given 4,000 pounds to produce it.[12]

This play was transferred to the West End where it had a lengthy run and then went on to Broadway where it starred Angela Lansbury. Where most people avoid stigma, Littlewood invested in the politics of stigma and thrived.

In her book *Underdogs,* Heather Love draws on this relationship between stigma and the field of queer studies. She specifically addresses Sedgewick's queer identification as well as its impact on the field.

It is clear from Sedgwick's reflections that identification across difference is fundamental to queer thought, and that it has always been controversial. Solidarity, though hardly simple, is at the origin of the field. The vision of a queer community of outsiders is driven by Sedgwick's complex identification with gayness, and as a gay man.[13]

In 2019, Lauren Berlant edited a book of essays titled *Reading Sedgwick.* In the introduction by Ramzi Fawaz, titled "*'An Open Mesh of Possibilities': The Necessity of Eve Sedgwick in Dark Times,*" Fawaz articulates the necessity of Sedgwick's work,

I say that Sedgwick *has a heart* for the universal, then, because she sees it as a contingent and hence intellectually imaginative space where, even if for a moment, we posit something wildly shared among us so that we can create a sense of collective reality and belonging, and where we might offer alternative universals to the existing ones proffered by liberal society that delimit our capacity to be otherwise.[14]

This was also a strength of Littlewood; she also had a heart for the universal. Her practice was modeled through her encounters with her collaborators. Her universal was performed in the ensemble and the role of the individual inside of it. "I really do believe in the community," she said. "I really do believe in the genius in every person. And I've heard that greatness come out of them, that great thing which is in people. And that's not romanticism, d'you see?"[15]

Lesson from Behan and the Impossibility of the Auteur

We are not always aware of our influences or even who we are listening to as we go about our work. Take, for example, this anecdote of my first experience of Littlewood. It wasn't until I was preparing to write this essay and was reading the biography *Joan Littlewood: Dreams and Realities,* which describes many of her projects in great detail, that I realized I *did* know the work of Joan Littlewood. I had been working on a project in graduate school that made me interested in accents and how actors learned them. I borrowed a box of cassettes from our voice professor, accent tutorials. At the time, I only had a cassette player in my car, so I listened to the tapes whenever I was driving. One of the cassettes turned out not to be an accent lesson but was a recording of the Broadway musical version of Littlewood's production of Behan's *The Hostage.* I assume it was in the box because it was a good example of an Irish accent. I left it my car cassette player for weeks and listened to it repeatedly. I loved it. It was such a strange musical; it undermined all of my assumptions and prejudices about musical theater. It was more play than musical, and as a bonus there were a few gay characters, and there were no heroes. It painted political conflict as a lonely sad trap that brutalized the common man. I finished my project and returned the cassettes and, I guess, forgot about the musical until reading the biography of Joan Littlewood. Here I learned that it was Littlewood who turned Behan's moving and empathetic play *The Hostage* into a gut-wrenching musical.

Littlewood had to be dogged with Behan, who struggled with alcoholism. She refused to let him abandon his play *The Hostage*. Littlewood made every effort to help him get the play written and then took what she felt was an unfinished work and developed it through improvisation with Behan and the cast. Holdsworth describes the process really as one of Littlewood salvaging scraps of Behan's brilliant mind.

> As Behan struggled with alcoholism and greater desire for the conviviality of the bar. Rather than putting his art for storytelling and witty dialogue on the page, Littlewood received only small sections of text to work with. Hence, she developed *The Hostage* in a haphazard way using Behan's text as a basis, bolstered by noting, and having others note, Behan's drunken anecdotes and vast repertoire of original, folk and music-hall songs by filling the gaps with improvisation. The result was a freewheeling tragi-comedy populated by eccentrics, prostitutes, pimps, a secret agent, a religious zealot and IRA sympathizers who share their songs, stories and coarse banter with the audience. The critics loved it. . .[16]

Like *The Quare Fellow* and *A Touch of Honey, The Hostage* was transferred to the West End and eventually to Broadway.

Littlewood's ingenuity and her ability to pick up a story, a problem, a person and make them seen (and adored) is stunning. This last sequence of her career, her years of working with Behan and Delaney and her success on the West End and then Broadway, dumbfounded me. Joan Littlewood had transferred four very significant works to Broadway in the late 50s, and yet she is absent from the American theater makers' imagination.

Why do you think this is?

I think it has everything to do with her underdog, or we could say marginal, or, let me assert, *quare* status. In her obituary, *The Guardian* describes her as "one of the bonniest fighters and intractably cussed personalities the theatre has known."[17] But this also has everything to do with the gatekeepers of culture. Throughout her career she and company members were frequently displaced; successful projects were censored and closed; and they were always underfunded. Their great achievements often were met with severe backlash. In 1958, Gerry Raffles, the Theatre Workshop manager, described the predicament as follows:

> As for The Arts Council, they have never believed that a theatre could be a success anywhere but in a respectable middle-class district, and our survival for ten years without their help and three years with their tiny grant has been a source of amazement, if not irritation, to them. They gave us no help at all until the Parisian critics acclaimed us.[18]

But it is *The Observer's* obituary of Brendan Behan in 1964 that gives us the best clue. For one, Joan Littlewood is never mentioned by name in the obit. But worse than that

Behan himself is insulted and humiliated by the author of the obituary. It begins with the cruel line, "Brendan Behan's death was a tragic waste, but his talent had long been destroyed by success and alcohol."[19] And it ends with, "The waste was incalculable." In the article, Behan is not mourned, but mocked, for his wasted talent and in the same breath "excused" for his existence. According to the obituary,

> Behan was ill-equipped by his upbringing to take care of his talent. His working-class childhood, with its motto of "If you've got it, spend it", followed by his war-time imprisonment for IRA activities, left him without any habit of self-discipline as a writer.[20]

I imagine that these are the very things that Joan loved about him. The writer of the obit not only buries Littlewood's role in Behan's life, he goes on to attack her influence: he blames Behan's success for his downfall – a success that has everything to do with Littlewood's dedication to his story. After praising *The Quare Fellow* for its "passionately humane attack on the degradation of the prison system itself," the obituary writer then diminishes the rest of Behan's work, which is in many ways also Littlewood's.

> None of Behan's other works preserves this element of Swiftian indignation – perhaps because the direction of his talent lay too much towards anarchic comedy. The Quare Fellow was an uncharacteristically naturalistic work: in The Hostage, his most popular play, he broke down the theatrical categories altogether, using an IRA incident for an extravaganza combining melodrama, farce, fantasy and ballad opera.[21]

Behan like Littlewood serves as an irritant to the gatekeepers of culture. Where Behan's stigma was his alcoholism and lack of self-discipline, that bonny cussed Littlewood was unrelenting in her ambitions. Littlewood carried many others with her on that journey.

Frogger

What do Joan Littlewood and the little frog in 1980s video game Frogger have in common? The answer is not that they are both forgotten or that they belong to another era.

The emergence of video game consoles for the home occurred around the period in my childhood when I was allowed to attend sleepovers. My friends and I spent the weekends sitting up all night playing Atari's Frogger between sneaking out for midnight bike rides and making some creepy attempts at communicating with the dead through a Ouija Board I found in my grandmother's "junk room." In Frogger, the aim was to maneuver a little frog across many lanes of traffic without getting splattered on the pavement. You advanced in the game through basic choices around timing and direction. You avoided oncoming trucks and cars by beating them out or waiting them out; but the obstacles grew in density, so your choices demanded a kind of dexterity of direction and tempo.

Like the frog, Joan Littlewood conceived of a destiny and went for it. But getting there meant crossing others' paths that seemed to follow a relentlessly straight road; it meant crossing others that might just squash you simply because you were in the way. And maybe, like the frog, Joan had many lives and learned from her relentless drive. And maybe, as she improved, the rules also changed – and maybe the rules improved. Perhaps even the goals changed, or the stakes got higher. Still, the only path forward meant navigating a system that might splatter you all over the pavement. To advance, the frog leaps, swerves, and adjusts to create her own jagged queer path – all the while accumulating knowledge that might make it easier the next time because she will have to start over again and again. And each success brings more difficult challenges.

Joan's legacy is complicated by ideas of success and failure because, for her, I think they were one and the same. For Joan, public success came with money and some fame. It also placed constraints on her process and her politics, thus foreclosing her ability to be innovative and to take risks. Success ultimately disappointed her enough that it instigated her quitting directing. Maybe that doesn't make for a good story: that things are left unfinished and that the West End and Broadway were never the aim. Maybe the story is deeply disappointing because of the tireless work of it all or because she never let it be easy. Or maybe she remains mostly absent from dominant narratives of theater legacies because she was a strong-willed woman who dressed like a man. Or it might just be that fame was never her goal. Her goal was to tell important stories by devising techniques for the theater that would have the greatest impact on the audience. Her goal was to "stop the waste of human ability" in the theater.

I'll Be More Help

I'll end this essay with Joan's offer. Because I think she did anticipate having a legacy, Joan wrote an autobiography. In her introduction to *Joan's Book,* she concludes with this note:

> Young actors and actresses, don't be puppets any longer! The directors and the critics won't help you; in television, film or the theatre they ask for the dregs of the old acting, mere 'expression', exploitation of your 'type'. In Shaftsbury Avenue or in the Brecht theatre, it's all the same. The theatre should be made up of individuals, not pawns. Keep your wits, develop your talent, take over the theatre, which now belongs to the managers or the landlords. Let's stop this waste of human ability. I have tried, for nearly twenty-seven years. I've had my nose to the grindstone and I'm still, comparatively speaking, alive. I'll be back. I'll be more help. – Joan Littlewood September 1961.[22]

Notes

1 Joan Littlewood, *Joan's Book* (London: Bloomsbury, 4th Edition, 2016), 14.
2 John Ezard and Michael Billington, *Joan Littlewood* (Obituary), *The Guardian* website September 23, 2002.
3 Nadine Holdsworth, *Joan Littlewood* from the *Routledge Performance Practitioners* (London: Routledge, 2006), 1.
4 Ibid., 10.
5 *Who Is Joan Littlewood.* Retrieved from https://www.rsc.org.uk/miss-littlewood/joan-littlewood-rebel-with-a-cause.
6 John Ezard and Michael Billington, *Joan Littlewood* (Obituary), *The Guardian* website September 23, 2002.
7 Nadine Holdsworth, *Joan Littlewood* from the *Routledge Performance Practitioners* (London: Routledge, 2006), 32.
8 Ibid., 33.
9 Phil Cleaves interview with Nadine Holdsworth for *Essential Drama. Com.* Retrieved from https://essentialdrama.com/practitioners/joan-littlewood/

10 Nadine Holdsworth, *Joan Littlewood* from the *Routledge Performance Practitioners* (London: Routledge, 2006), 20.
11 Joan Littlewood, *Joan's Book* (London: Bloomsbury, 4th Edition, 2016), 374–375.
12 Ibid.
13 Heather Love, *Underdogs* (Chicago and London: The University of Chicago Press, 2021), 169.
14 Ramzi Fawaz, "'An Open Mesh of Possibilities': The Necessity if Eve Sedgwick in Dark Times," in *Reading Sedgwick* edited by Lauren Berlant (Durham: Duke University Press, 2019), 13.
15 John Ezard and Michael Billington, *Joan Littlewood* (Obituary), *The Guardian* website September 23, 2002.
16 Nadine Holdsworth, *Joan Littlewood* from the *Routledge Performance Practitioners* (London: Routledge, 2006), 30.
17 John Ezard and Michael Billington, *Joan Littlewood* (Obituary), *The Guardian* website September 23, 2002.
18 Joan Littlewood, *Joan's Book* (London: Bloomsbury, 4th Edition, 2016), 374.
19 Irving Wardle, *From the Observer archive: 22 March 1964: the sad death of Brendan Behan. The Guardian* website March 22, 2014.
20 Ibid.
21 Ibid.
22 Joan Littlewood, *Joan's Book* (London: Bloomsbury, 4th Edition, 2016), 16.

Essay Five

ACTORS! LET THEM BE ASTONISHING

The Astonished Actor

I love actors. Perhaps it is helpful to state the obvious: you can't direct without actors. The entire process of making a show relies on the actors' willingness to show up, to be present, and consistent. They're also expected to be dynamic and beautiful and real or funny or radiant. The great queer auteur director Joe Chaikin wrote a book about his practice called *The Presence of the Actor*. The word **presence** is so key to naming the relationships between actors and between actors and their audience. I was introduced to Chaikin's book when I was 18, at the very moment I was discovering I might like theater more than math and engineering. The book was written in 1973, the year I was born. The person who introduced me to the book also helped me understand that I definitely liked women, as I was so taken with her. That attraction, that explosion of desire, both physical and intellectual, happened while I was reading Chaikin's book, which I suppose is why nuggets from the book have lodged themselves permanently in my psyche. In the 30 years since that first encounter, I have inscribed Chaikin's ideas into my directing practice, reworking some of them as my own. What has stayed with me the most from my introduction to *The Presence of the Actor* is Chaikin's assertion that actors must be in contact with their sense of astonishment and that the power of theater depends on the actors' ability to be present to their own experiences; they should not just indulge their "popular feelings" but should be present to experiences that shock us.[1] If this works, it can be astonishing.

Real Lesbians, Not Actors

The disclaimer "real people, not actors" makes a familiar appearance across the bottom of the screen on many television commercials. The first time I saw this disclaimer I was startled. What caught me by surprise was its implication that actors are not "real people." The sentiment itself is not surprising, but its weirdly blatant pronouncement, "real people, not actors," confirms the prejudice people have against actors. It also confirms

DOI: 10.4324/9781003253402-6

the prejudice we may hold against "real people." Actors are unreal and real people are what? Honest? Unadorned? Human? I'm curious what that distinction is meant to make us think or feel.

If actors are not real people, what are they? If you are acting, are you an actor? Are we supposed to imagine that these "real people" acting in a commercial are in fact real customers or real users of the product or just that they are untrained actors? Actors without headshots? People who don't look like actors? Actors without awe? People who aren't awesome?

I suppose a person is real because they are not artificial or phony or something worse, like liars. I have too often experienced artists and filmmakers boast about working with "non-actors." It is not unusual to hear artists who use live performers or make films profess disdain for actors. They will proudly assert: "I don't use actors in my work." Why? What is the distinction? Or what is better about a non-actor or a real person?

This idea of divorcing the task from the person is totally fascinating to me. Maybe because I am a teacher and, more often than not, I work with people who have little experience with acting but, nevertheless, are required to "act." They want to act. They want to be good actors. There are so many people in this world who would like to act. I have a neighbor named Michael who is a 73-year-old gay, black landscaper. He landscapes many of the yards on our street and on the surrounding blocks. He is a treasure of West Philadelphia. I love doing my own gardening, but I always search him out when I have questions about my yard, dividing plants, getting rid of pesky plants, etc. Michael hands out advice freely, but more than once he has asked me when I will give him acting lessons. He wants to act. He has now assembled a list of folks in our neighborhood who want to act. All of these neighbors, these real people, want to act. They want to rent a room in a church basement and get to work. Not because they want to be something other than real, but because they want to be real in new ways, they want to inhabit their own bodies and minds on other levels of awareness or inside of other imagined circumstances. For them this is would be pleasurable.

I'll concede that not all people who act are actors, like not all people who run are runners or all people who do DIY home plumbing repairs are plumbers. Maybe we could use the phrase "DIY actors, not real actors."

Consider these two phrases: "Real lesbians, not actors" and "Actors, not real lesbians."

"Actors, not real lesbians" had been the norm for so long. (*Real lesbians* could be replaced with *real transfolk, real native people, real Muslims, real women over the age of 60 who aren't Meryl Streep, stocky women, men with high-pitched voices, complicated black women, Japanese Americans, Brooke's neighbors,* and on and on.)

People didn't just dream up "real people" as the opposite of "actors." They are responding to the industry's norms and aesthetics. Norms that say actors can play anyone. Norms that say you need to have a certain kind of appeal or energy or presence to be an actor. Maybe there is a special quality that good actors bring to the stage. But something else is also happening – something that has conditioned us to believe that actors look and behave with a certain kind of. . . .Ahhh, what is it? I have been struggling to put this into words. Maybe because it varies by gender?

I have repeatedly witnessed very good actors develop plays with playwrights and theaters, only to be replaced when the play converts to more "high-stakes," broad-appeal venues. The industry has set in place a standard that appears to be more about brand, aesthetics, and normativity than about talent or even genuineness. I have watched a play written by a transman about transmen staring trans and gender queer actors, recast with (often small-framed) cis-men and cis-women lesbian (who are already famous for some role they played on television before they "came out") when the play moved to a more commercial theater. Perhaps a choice like that might face pushback in this current climate, but the persistence of this norm and prejudice is old and runs deep.

What I am saying is – as frustrating as I find this sentiment about real people – we cannot fault those who long for real people. Because they long for something they have not seen enough of on the stage or on the screen. At least not in leading roles. Actors occupy a place of desire and relation for us. This impulse toward desire and attraction is not the problem. The problem is that what has been constructed as desirable is really just conforming to the desire(s) of small handful of people with power.

Actors, Not Real Lesbians

Take for example these hunks. I was ten years old when the film *The Outsiders* came out. I could not take my eyes off these boys and men. I saved my money for teen magazines like *Tiger Beat*[2] and *Seventeen*[3] so I could devour images of them. Look at them! And then picture them as I did as a ten-year-old, as the woman I wanted to be and to be with. They are so HOT (Figure 5.1).

FIGURE 5.1 Promotional photo for the film *The Outsiders* released in 1983.

Imagine a woman version of Emilio Estevez. She would be the woman little Alison sings about in the song "Ring of Keys" from Lisa Kron's musical version of Alison Bechtel's *Fun Home*. This promo photo could easily be a picture of the butch faction of a lesbian commune from the 1980s, except the lesbians have been replaced by young men who will sky rocket to stardom. When my tween self-imagined kissing somebody, I imagined myself as Ponyboy (C. Thomas Howell) doing the kissing. But I must say my Ponyboy would have kissed that Johnny (Ralph Macchio) – especially if she were a girl.

The point is, I could conjure in these actors something I desired. But for me it took translation, invention. I can't imagine how my life would have been different if there were women in films who looked like this.

When we think about desire, our first impulse is to think of the pleasures of wanting another. But desire is also about wanting to be another. That person is so deliciously beautiful, I want to be them. My friend the actor Jess Barbagallo differentiates these two desires as one of libido and one of narcissism. (And Freud calls them identification and desire. I want to be/I want to have.) Actors occupy these places for us; they fill the roles in the stories we watch. We consume so much "experience" through actors.

Don't Act! Do Act! Act Well!

Acting is difficult work that demands rigor, intelligence, openness, and vulnerability.

The actor and writer Heidi Schreck once told me the playwright Mac Wellman told her during auditions for one of his plays, that it is always better when actors just don't act. He said something like, "I wish they would stop acting and just say the words." Heidi then told me that Mac doesn't actually want actors not to act, he wants actors to be good actors. According to Heidi good actors look like they are doing nothing; they appear to be wandering through the world experiencing it and reacting to it. When they speak the text, it's like they are just saying the words – like they might say them. They appear to be real people.

This is an old anecdote that was passed on to me. Heidi carried it around and then passed it to me, and now I also carry it around and share it with others. The story recalls the many biases against actors and the perplexing standards we create for them. Don't act! Do act! Act well!

There are instances when actors should appear everyday, even mundane, and other times where they must appear to be extraordinary people where the feat of acting feels palpable or even athletic. Actors understand these contradictions. Actors agree to this scrutiny. They agree to the vulnerability these conditions create. Building a career in acting is a risky venture. It is an art that needs to be honed and developed. It is an art that indulges intimacy. Also, acting education is not cheap. The work of establishing a career and being seen is often quite debasing or exploitative. It demands long periods of deep uncertainty about your ability to provide for yourself. It asks you to have a kind of faith or hope and a sense of self-worth that is hard to maintain in a field that takes your openness as cue for abuse.

People don't usually like vulnerable people. People don't feel comfortable with risk takers. Actors must be both.

Good Actors

When discussing actors, real actors, trained actors and the objectification of actors, I find myself and others throwing around the word "good." Even earlier in this essay, I casually drop the word good in this sentence: "Maybe there is a special quality that **good** actors bring to the stage."

This idea of the good actor becomes tricky or sticky. You could say that, yes, you are certainly an actor if you learn your lines and go on the stage and say them; but are you a good actor? What makes you good? Doesn't being a good actor matter? Who determines who is a good actor and how?

In the final series of essays in this book, *The Education of the Director*, I assert that the director bears the brunt of the responsibility for the actor having a good performance. The actor's ability to be good is deeply dependent on the conditions that are created for them. I shared an early draft of this essay with Jess Barbagallo, whom I have directed in numerous projects and have collaborated with on *Room for Cream*. He also pressed me on how good acting comes into these concerns:

> Hey B-
>
> Really enjoyed reading this. I'm wondering about audience here. As a person who knows theater, I feel as though I'm being directly spoken to. I guess this is a guidebook for young directors. . . do you think you will use anecdotes, or does that feel silly to you? I remember you once asking me why I was laughing or what I was doing with my face, probably when we were working on Macbeth. I think you were trying to question some blocks/defenses in Jess, not the character. So, I wonder if you can talk about that, not me per se, but what makes this unified company? I know it's not about neutrality. I know you care about good acting and like to watch a performer shine, but don't want one person to overtake the stage. That's how I read your casting or how your productions feel. . . are there other good ways?
>
> xo,
> Jess[4]

I will confess that I feel genuinely insecure about determining who is a good actor. And this is because I know that my response to actors is bound up in my own affection for a person or my own thrill in their choices. And this happens at all levels of work with actors. Sometimes when I am teaching the course Introduction to Acting, a kind of shy, awkward and soft-spoken student just lands on something in a scene; and I can feel the whole class sucked in, appreciative, moved. And I feel like, "Wow, that was so **good**." But that feeling is always laced with doubt because I have been in a room too often with artists who genuinely get hostile about an actor's performance. I collaborated with someone who, for years, would sit with me over a beer after rehearsals and just rip the actors to shreds. But I was thinking, "Really, are they that bad?" What is he looking at? I didn't argue back, but I was always shocked and pained by his critique. I loved the actors, and I liked the things they did that were not the obvious choices; my impulse was actually to nurture and cultivate those very same perceived flaws. Ah, maybe those *flaws* read to me as something *real* and *good*.

I do have lots of opinions about every little detail and choice in a scene; I'm a director! I watch for choices like a hawk and constantly filter what to make a note about and what to let go – for the time being, knowing that the actor, too, is just trying things out. I feel strongly about choices, choices on every level, but I separate that from goodness and badness as a whole. I love it when actors make me hear all the words, when they get the nuances of a scene. I like it when they don't show me what is happening but instead invite me to crawl up inside that moment with them. But then I also like it when they surprise me with something so big and dramatic and explosive that it's as if their performance leaves a print on my body.

I think about acting a lot. If you were to make a pie chart of the things that I spent time thinking about these last 30 years, I think the biggest slice of the pie might actually be acting. Yet, I don't trust that what I think is good is what other people think is good. I am definitely more generous than your average person about acting. Which may seem like a fatal or tragic flaw in a director.

But on the flip side, my fine attention to detail and the intensity of my watching and listening gives me an ability to pinpoint where actors might become disconnected or stuck in a choice that draws them away from the others' offerings. The aspiration is that working this way draws out the strengths in the performers but will also create conditions of positive exposure. By positive exposure, I mean that actors can draw out or expose the best in one another.

The Noh actor Zeami (1363–1443) describes this condition in his treatise titled "Learning the Way" (Shūdōsho).

> The actors who participate in any particular performance must of course work to perfect their individual skills, but there is another principle as well to which they must give the most earnest consideration. In order for them to create the impression of a truly successful and complete performance, the various skills of all the performers must be harmonized together. If their various accomplishments are not blended in this fashion, then no matter how skillfully they may perform on an individual basis, neither their dance or their song will seem united and capable of creating a sense of completeness. Rather, the performers must work for the creation in themselves of a fundamental attitude of mutual concession and cooperation in order to manifest properly their skills in dancing and singing. No one must take the attitude that he alone can succeed through his own individual skill.[5]

I return regularly to the practice of Zeami when considering the work of the actor. This is, in part, because the unique vocabulary he uses in his description of the actor's skill. He attempts to describe and define the intangibles of acting.

In his treatise "The True Path of the Flower" (written in the 1420), Zeami writes extensively on the fundamentals of the actor's art. He breaks these fundamentals down into Skin, Flesh and Bone. He describes Bone as "the exceptional artistic strength that a gifted actor shows naturally in his performance" which arrives from an *inborn ability*.[6] Flesh is the visible element of a performance that "arises from the power of the skills that the actor has obtained by mastering the Two Basic Arts of chant and dance."[7] Skin is the ease and beauty "obtained when the other two elements are thoroughly perfected."[8] He is circling around the forever questions: Does talent make a great actor? Does hard work and training do this? Is it a combination? Must you have both?

But the thing that strikes me about Zeami is that he always ties these qualities back into how the actor is perceived by the audience. The *Flower* is the audience's experience of an actor's performance as novel and fresh.[9] The *flower* somehow makes the most sense to me because of the variety of flowers, because of the range of beauty of a flower, because of the uniqueness and familiarity of them, AND because I personally am very moved by the beauty of flowers. Sometimes the more unique and strange the more they move me, or sometimes flowers in sheer mass are overwhelmingly stunning, or some combinations of flowers can evoke something exciting and stimulating. And for Zeami it is the fleeting nature, the stunning appearance coupled with the sureness that it will wither. Catching sight of something in the right moment. An actor that gives you that feeling, no matter how fleeting, is likely a good actor.

Actors to Directors

Drawing Zeami into this conversation also allows for us to consider more deeply the complexities of the relationship between the director and the actor. The lineage of the director is really from that of the lead actor. This is true in both Western and Eastern theater traditions. In his treatise Zeami conceives of himself as an actor writing about acting. But Zeami was also the leader of his company. He is credited with transforming Noh from "country entertainment. . . into a superb total theatrical experience. . . in order to produce for his audiences an experience of profundity and almost religious exhilaration."[10] I won't go over the history of Zeami here, but what I am pointing to is Zeami's role as both the leader of his Noh company and its lead actor. Noh companies were competitive troupes that vied for support from shogunates. Because of the highly competitive nature of the art, their training was kept secretive and only passed down from actor to actor. Roles were taught through repetition and imitation. It was only after you could replicate the role with precision that you could then, if you were skilled enough, alter the role with signature choices. The unique acting style of each troupe determined their artistic worth. But Zeami, as the lead actor and thus company leader, was compelled to not only teach young actors through the traditional body to body passing on of a role, but to detail the work through a written treatise. The treatise was never meant to be read or shared by people outside of the troupe; it was meant for the "legacy of his descendants" to remind them of the *true path* of the art.[11] Zeami's description of the elements of the art of acting is an invaluable precursor to the efforts of the first directors to codify the training of the actor.

The director did not become a dominant force in the theater until the end of the nineteenth century. For decades, if not centuries, theater was built around the playwright and the actor/manager. Training was informal; theaters relied on older actors to provide mentoring for younger actors. In the US, theater companies were dominated by a star-system in which "stars could divide their time among several companies, creating financial success for all."[12] As the position of director developed, actor training began in earnest in Western theater. Directors were the first theater artists to start acting schools. The director shaped the good actor. Directors devised common practices for approaching text and character. They built strategies through observation of actors in rehearsal; they identified choices that actors made that were repeatable and could transfer to others across an array of conditions.

I imagine early acting companies throughout the world as similar in approach to jazz ensembles that are built around a star. Zeami's role was not unlike John Coltrane's for example. Like Coltrane, for each performance Zeami set the tone, read the crowd, and guided the performance. Everything that happened on stage was made manifest through his interpretation. Decisions about energy, tempo, and length of performance were made live and in real time by Zeami. But did Zeami respond to the other performers? Was there a passing of energy when someone else was feeling the "hot hand" (*that's a basketball term for when a shooter just can't miss*)? Coltrane was certainly responding to the other musicians in the room. He was so phenomenal, but also aware that he was made better through the dynamic within his ensembles. My friend Ross would intervene here and say this is maybe a little different from him setting the tone. He'd remind us of when "Coltrane and Elvin Jones would go to outer space together."[13] Coltrane is no longer running that room but is experiencing a profound listening, a listening that probably troubles the idea of the one running the room. And the audience is actually witnessing this moment of performers listening to each other and also listening to each other's listening to the room, the audience, the world.

I shared this Coltrane comparison with a playwright friend who has since told me that he would like theater to be like that. He wants to consider what it would mean to write a play for an actor who is like an impresario band leader – someone like John Coltrane. He wants to consider how you write for an actor who dictates in real time how the language moves through time and space, who can respond to the energy of the room and guide the cast through that journey with the audience. Can the director make this dynamic possible?

The Actor and Their Auteur

The relationship between the actor and the auteur director is one of the most special in the theater. It might be something akin to children inventing a special language that guides their imaginary play. The auteur creates an environment or frame or structure that gives permission for dynamic play. Ideally the auteurs process contains enough structure and clear process or methods that the actors can feel both secure and free to explore.

In the previous essay *Who is Joan Littlewood?* I closed with an offer Littlewood makes in an address to "young actors and actresses." She asks them to keep their wits, develop their talent, and take over the theater. "Let's stop this waste of human ability," she writes in response to what she sees as the misuse of the actor. And she ends with the promise, "I'll be more help."[14]

I highlighted the phrase "I'll be more help" as a kind of button on the essay because I want you take that up, to consider how Littlewood even now could be more help to you.

This letter is the conclusion of the introduction to her biography *Joan's Book*. What is curious is the specificity of the address; she is not addressing audiences, the public or playwrights, even though she spent much of her career cultivating her relationships with them. She addresses the actor whom she worries is betrayed and abused by the field. She obviously understands the necessity of the powerful, beautiful, brilliant, sexy, scary, and vulnerable actor. It was the actor who joined in her explorations of Stanislavsky's system, and Laban Technique, and Meyerhold's Biomechanics. It was the actor who willingly improvised incomplete plays to draw the material forward. The actor is the skin, bone, and flesh, whose ability to be present and experience awe makes the experience novel and fresh. We are nothing without the actor.

Yet, each of us will work differently with actors. We will develop our own practices that rely on their commitment and openness. This isn't easy work; it demands the cultivation of trust and shared aesthetics or politics. But what matters is that we can build a process for actors that makes it possible for them all to be good, all to be stunning and delectable. We can make shows that reveal their individual strengths and their beauty while also supporting them to build a dynamic together.

Auteurs I Know

When I moved to New York as a young director, there were three prominent queer auteurs who demonstrated for me the wildly different ways that one could build a practice with actors. They were Anne Bogart of the SITI Company, Marianne Weems of Builders' Association, and John Jesurun. And though their work asks for radically different approaches from the actor, it was not uncommon for actors to work with more than one of these directors.

Anne Bogart, who is arguably the US' most established lesbian auteur director, runs a theater company that trains its own actors (SITI). She ran the Saratoga International Theater Institute with the Japanese auteur Tadashi Suzuki where they trained actors in Viewpoints and Suzuki Method. Bogart also heads a graduate directing program and, therefore, trains American directors. She has built a successful company around a repertoire of shows using an ensemble trained in the movement and composition based methods of Viewpoints and Suzuki. Like Littlewood, Bogart sometimes made original shows devised with an acting ensemble built around a theme, or biography, or story; other times she worked with living playwrights; and other times she directed known classic plays. But she always built her shows by using an ensemble trained in her methods.

Marianne Weems, however, works completely differently with actors in the Builders' Association. She relies less on training and more on the facilitation of a core group of collaborators who bring their own skills and vocabularies to the process. Weems works with more technologies and over lengthier development periods. She has worked with a core group of actors for years. Still, new actors and artists will join for new shows, but those new actors do not necessarily have to learn a new practice, they instead have to learn how their own practice can be in conversation with all of the artists in the room. Weems describes the practice in her introduction to The Builders' Association Book:

> All of this is to say that much of this work began on the edges of "the theater," and the artists who still comprise the company came largely from outside the theater with expertise in other media. That's what makes being in the room interesting. The point of beginning with *everyone* involved, and with all of their tools, is that each element brings its own language to the core idea, and each informs the entirety of the production. The designers are there with their tools to frame or magnify or influence a way that an actor is delivering a line, the actors are there to play with their performance to a camera and on stage at the same time, we all circle around the key concept, looking for the moment when it all clicks.[15]

Weems asks the actor to enter her projects with their own language and make sense of themselves as artists among all the other languages being employed in the room. Actor Moe Angeles describes the experience as a kind of learning-while-doing, or relearning-while-doing:

> I struggled mightily at first to follow the "story" of XTRAVAGANZA. There were two problems with my approach, one being that I was looking for some traditional narrative hook to drag my sorry self through the show and this hook was going to require some work to find and I am essentially lazy. Secondly, I was looking for said hook in the wrong haystack, in the more conventional performer haystack of some sort of

connection with my fellow performers, formed because of what emotional journey we were passing through onstage.

The great lesson I learned doing that show was that Marianne was telling these stories through a visual language in conjunction with the more traditional theatrics of scenes of dialogue between characters that further a plot. The pictures, the video, the media were also telling the story. This is patently obvious to anyone who has seen a Builders' show but it is anything but clear if you are one of the humans running around *in* that show.[16]

The auteur writer/director John Jesurun also uses live video and acting for the camera in his staged plays and his live serial drama *Chang in a Void Moon*. But Jesurun relies heavily on a kind of style. In my experience, it almost feels like a full-throttled attack on the words. These words are his own and written to absorb his approach to acting. Jesurun builds into his texts a tempo, but also directs the actors to resist dramatic reading. One actor described it as "fast and flat."

"'Fast and flat' was Jesurun's preferred acting style, which went well with the minimalist staging, and while there were exceptions to this method, a minimum of emotion at maximum speed could be helpful in getting through a typical script."[17]

This style, however, was effective and surprising. It created room for little pockets or openings to some other dynamic – or to explosive emotion. Jesurun explained this almost as a disruption of emotion that occurred despite the approach being technical, crisp, and fast.

JJ. . . . To me, there's an overall sense of 'emotionality' that you can convey by having people act in the way that I have them act. Then at certain points let them become very emotional. It cuts right through the acting facade of putting on an emotion. Somebody's going along and this burst of emotion comes out and it comes out to you as much more raw. I think it's more striking than the overly-paced, breathy kind of styles that to me are so boring. The actors altogether form something that's very emotional, but not in an overt way. All working together and speaking in certain rhythms. It builds up some kind of emotion. But I think people tend to look at individual actors and expect that they 'move' the audience in a way that they've expected to be moved in. You know people want to be performed for in that individual way. They want to latch on to a particular character, to feel as that character feels. Which I think gets off the point.[18]

I choose these directors because their work with actors and collaborators strikes me as the thing itself – as the essence of the project. Upon seeing their shows, I am less stricken by the narrative, but by the way the event or story arises out of the performance. I am moved by the people and the way they inhabit a shared way of working and relation. I am drawn into a world built by many voices that have joined together in a shared vision. This is what actors are capable of. If you let them be that – or you make a room that allows for something to be real, not because it is not fake or a lie, but because it is built out of a shared way or working together in the room, on a script, or through a process. The success and influence of these directors has surely paved the way for queer auteurs as it has for me. But instead of pointing to a concise method of working that you should replicate to be a great auteur director, their work reveals that their approaches are bound up in their process and their relationships with collaborators.

See Them, Love Them, and Let Them (Be)

Somewhere I read that actors are heroes. This seems correct to me. Actors are willing to take big risks and give themselves over to the role, the whims of the writer or director, the desire of the audience. That they give of themselves in such a public way makes them easy targets for harsh critique and pathologizing. It is fair play to discuss actors as divas or pretenders or fakes and, sometimes even, as untrustworthy. But this is confounding to me and, I would hope, to anybody who has been in the rehearsal room with actors.

In the rehearsal room, the actors' agreement with the director and one another is that they are totally present and available. They are willing to do the same thing over and over again. They are willing to be told, "No, that doesn't work. Try something else." They are willing to bring their whole intellect and bodily knowledge, without holding anything back. Through their desire to engage the role, they bring vulnerability as well as generosity into the room. They give and give and give of themselves while at the same time following the director.

As a result of their public facing role, actors are objectified, scrutinized, and sexualized – by our industry, by casting directors, by producers, by us, and by audiences. And they know it. So how do we take that seriously? What drives a person to agree to being so objectified? We take it seriously by loving them. We value them by desiring them and knowing that they are not mistaken that they are desired and that people want to see them and have deep experiences through them.

As a director, this relationship, your relationship with the actors you work with, is your primary relationship. If you cannot keep these relationships healthy, then you should not do this work. Because, more than anybody in your collaboration, it is the actors who are reaching into space to make meaning with the audience.

Remember, this is not a "how to" book or a "do it like me and you will be an incredible director" book; but this feels important to share. When I begin a rehearsal, I make a promise to my actors that I will not let them look bad, that I will not humiliate them, that I will listen to them and see them. Even though I will push them and challenge them, I will not ask them to be uncomfortable or afraid on the stage. I make this promise because I cannot bear the idea of these beautiful, generous people feeling shame, embarrassment, or humiliation. But also, it is just as true, the work is only powerful if the actors have the freedom to find their strength, to be brilliant and also vulnerable. This is their gift to us.

You don't have to run a company of actors, or have been credited for harnessing the work of Viewpoints, or have founded an institute, or spearheaded a graduate program to be an auteur. You just need to know how to work with actors, how to relate to your audience, how to read texts. Being an auteur director is about a kind of care and comfort with the theater you want to make. It is about holding and nurturing a vision. It is about having the knowledge, openness and empathy to lead your team there. It is about loving your actors and understanding that they will be objectified and about holding them in their power of seduction.

I think people imagine that the auteur is a genius; but from what I can tell, the auteur's strength of vision evolves through curiosity, openness, generosity, and rigor. And if you are a genius, well, then that is fine too. Just don't be an abusive one. You must care for your actors. You must nourish their ability to be astonished.

Notes

1 Joseph Chaikin, *The Presence of the Actor* (New York: Theatre Communications Group, 1991), 6–7.
2 *Tiger Beat* was a teen fan magazine marketed to adolescent girls in the 1965–1980s.
3 *Seventeen* was a consumer culture magazine marketed to adolescent girls, 1944–2010s.
4 Jess Barbagallo. Email to Brooke O'Harra. January 3, 2021.
5 Zeami translated by J. Thomas Rimer and Yamazaki Masakazu, "Learning the Way (Shūdōsho)," in *On the Art of the Nō Drama* (Princeton, NJ: Princeton University Press, 1984), 163.
6 Zeami translated by J. Thomas Rimer and Yamazaki Masakazu, "True Path of the Flower," in *On the Art of the Nō Drama* (Princeton, NJ: Princeton University Press, 1984), 69.
7 Ibid.
8 Ibid.
9 Zeami translated by J. Thomas Rimer and Yamazaki Masakazu, "Style of the Flower," in *On the Art of the Nō Drama* (Princeton, NJ: Princeton University Press, 1984), 53.
10 J. Thomas Rimer, "The Background of Zeami's Treatises," in *On the Art of the Nō Drama* (Princeton, NJ: Princeton University Press, 1984), ivii.
11 Zeami translated by J. Thomas Rimer and Yamazaki Masakazu, "Style and the Flower," in *On the Art of the Nō Drama* (Princeton, NJ: Princeton University Press, 1984), 37.
12 Arthur Bartow, "Introduction," in *Training of the American Actor* (New York: Theatre Communications Group, 2006), xvi.
13 Ross Gay, Email to Brooke O'Harra. March 6, 2022.
14 Joan Littlewood, *Joan's Book* (London: Bloomsbury, 4th Edition, 2016), 16.
15 Marianne Weems, *Forward* from the Final Draft of *The Builders Association Book* written by Shannon Jackson and Marianne Weems (Draft as of September 2, 2014), 9.
16 Moe Angelos, *ENDNOTES: Artist's Voice: Moe Angelos, performer/co-creator* from the Final Draft of *The Builders Association Book* written by Shannon Jackson and Marianne Weems (Draft as of September 2, 2014), 147.
17 Joe Hagan, *John Jesurun* in *Art Forum*, October 1999. Retrieved from https://www.artforum.com/print/199908/john-jesurun-843.
18 John Jesurun in an interview with Craig Gholson in *Bomb Magazine* January 1, 1985. Retrieved from https://bombmagazine.org/articles/john-jesurun/.

Essay Six

THE EDUCATION OF THE DIRECTOR (IN THREE PARTS)

Introduction to the Education of the Director

I'm not sure I could pinpoint the moment that my directing practice and my very real investments as a teacher and mentor collapsed into each other. When did these selves begin colluding and collaborating? What would I learn if I were to track back through the influence or the many little interventions into my practice that resulted from being introduced to artists and plays while teaching? For example, I learned about Joan Littlewood well into my career because I put her on my syllabus; now I can barely disentangle her motivations and approaches from my own.

While teaching *advanced scene study* at the Experimental Theater Wing of New York University's Tisch School, I was asked to teach experimental approaches in scene study; and this is when I began to explore the relationship between the Noh and Kabuki traditions of teaching *acting* * *(dance)* through the physical repetition of recorded movement (in this case we replicated unrelated performance we found in film – like spaghetti westerns or Frank Capra comedies of the 1940s). I became invested in exploring what common ideas could be found across seemingly disparate approaches to acting. I was doing this to help my students, but in fact these questions went on to occupy my own projects for years.

After teaching as an adjunct at Tisch for five years, I moved to a full-time position at the women's school Mt. Holyoke College,[1] located in Western Massachusetts near the famously lesbian town of Northampton. While there, I unabashedly let my investments and interests cross between the work I was doing with my company Two-headed Calf and the work I was doing with my students. I directed two student-plays a year while also developing new shows in New York City with my company; and, at the same time, I was running the live serial drama *Room for Cream* in the East Village (yet, it was set in a fictional lesbian/queer/trans town in Western Massachusetts – wink wink). I would sometimes bring the material I was working on in NYC to Mt. Holyoke for the students

---

* Acting is being called dance. For all intents and purposes, the artists mean Acting and Dance are interchangeable in Noh and Kabuki.

DOI: 10.4324/9781003253402-7

to workshop or try in class. When Two-headed Calf was working on the show *Trifles* by Susan Glaspell, I simultaneously directed it with students at MHC for their mainstage. It was not the same production; the Two-headed Calf show contained wordless songs and incorporated the ensemble Yarn/Wire. But the two productions informed each other; both casts were working with time and silence in relation to gender and power. To be honest, the student actors were sometimes more capable of taking the risk of stretching time through stillness than the professionals were; they could sustain difficult choices for longer.

During that period, I was able to build a space with students to explore ideas and take risks that I couldn't always take with professionals. Yet, the largest influence those students had on me was to open my mind to the idea of embracing spaces for women, for trans folks, and for queers. They introduced me to the possibility of making work directed toward their public, one that was different from other publics. They taught me that there was no space that was truly for everyone, so why pretend otherwise. I learned this from the uniqueness of the institution's "all-women" atmosphere as well as from the deep limitations the college community still maintained with regard to gender identity and race and religion and all the politics of identity that are real and that matter. I learned this through all the complex ways these students identified with one another and also disidentified (which was, often, as painful for them as it was empowering).

These 20 years of teaching and mentoring taught me the dangers of making assumptions about people and ideas. They showed me the thrill of being a beginner and of not having the answers. Teaching has motivated me to hover and indulge in the moments of not knowing. But it has demonstrated, by contrast, how little opportunity and support there is for a professional to work with the freedom to not know what you might be making. Wouldn't it be great if a producer simply asked you, "What are you curious about?" or "Do you wonder what might happen if. . .?" These are questions you can ask your students regularly. It is through teaching that I have learned to find space to engage my questions of the field. And maybe I am also making a dent in reimagining how we study theater and how we study directing in particular.

Still, teaching is disconcerting – because who am I to tell you how you should do something or to tell you what is correct. It is through my discomfort with this role that I have turned back toward my own questions and my own hopes for discovery. I am also learning to listen as my students attempt to convey their points of view; I am learning to recognize their resistances as openings to possibilities for more complicated theater in the US. Maybe they will seize permission to make theater that is messy and startling and not for everyone, or maybe they'll bring us a tidy and generous or delicate or gleeful theater. I mean, who knows what they could make?

THE EDUCATION OF THE DIRECTOR PART ONE: DOING DIRECTING

The only way to learn how to direct is by doing – **doing directing**. This is why teaching directing is so difficult.

Bear with me as I tell you about a scene this conjures for me, one that I never even witnessed first-hand. The scene emerges from an anecdote I was told about an acting professor's public unravelling as he retreated from art and community. *These things happen.* The scene was described like this,

> Finally, he brought chairs, desks and a chalkboard into the acting studio. After that, he only taught acting as a lecture course. I remember walking by the studio and looking in to see the students at desks. They were in desks! In the acting studio! Looking at a chalkboard that had 'ACTING is DOING' written across it.

It's this one particular image that remains so vivid. I can't help but worry that writing this essay on the *Education of the Director* is like me standing in front of you scrawling on a chalkboard: "DIRECTING is DOING."

Given the impossible task of teaching directing when most directing classes are comprised of "directors" but no actors, instructors often resort to teaching directing through an accumulation of skills and vocabulary. They spend a lot of time working on skills like *script analysis* or *blocking* and learning vocabulary like *upstage, downstage, in the round, posts, etc.* This translates into a "how-to" approach, into teaching directing as a craft. It lulls the students into believing that, if they do all those things as described, then the work will be interesting or inspired. This is also how norms become so entrenched.

I get it. Teaching is hard. There is a lot a pressure to have your students leave class thinking, "I learned this and this and this" – not simply saying, "I **did** this and this and this." The idea of achievement is so loaded and tricky. Praise starts to replace witnessing as a means of marking experience. People will say "I like that" instead of "I saw this." But praise can be a risky form of feedback; it can make things instantly stuck because, if something is supposedly good, then why would anyone change it or grow it or try it another way.

Directing ought to be taught in the form of lab classes that use a critique model. This is the model more commonly used in art courses. (*This might be good news if you are reading this essay and are not a student – because you can do this on your own, maybe by forming a collective or starting a kind of directing working group. You all can work independently on very short scenes then come together and share them – talk about them.*)

Because I believe in this method of study, I ask my students to bring fully directed, off-book scenes to class each week. They have to be short – starting with eight lines. By the third week, they can have up to 24 lines. After three weeks they switch to new plays and start over with eight-line scenes. The students have to find and recruit their own actors. These scenes start about 90 seconds in length and eventually grow to about 4 minutes. And in these few minutes the director can start to learn about the intricacies of the text, of their actors' impulses, of space, and of their relationship to audience.

This kind of class is a challenge to teach and to take. It is difficult for the students to find actors who will come to class multiple weeks in a row. (*Logistically it's hard to wrangle folks, but this is also a key to the challenge of directing. These relationships in all scenarios are socially, emotionally, and financially hard. Finding actors is not like going out and buying paint; it is about creating or sustaining relationships. These relationships are beautiful but also are at times burdensome).* Often my students' actors aren't trained actors and will have to be trained by the student director. (*Ultimately a good thing!*) But this approach is useful; it teaches a director to see all the details of their work. It teaches them how to work with actors. What becomes immediately clear is that there is so much for directors to think about or look at – like where they put the performance in relation to an audience, what they assume is clear about a text, how their actors read a script or relate to space, or how they even breathe.

In class, each student shows their own scene and then is given the opportunity to give their cast notes (in front of the class) and then shows it again. This can happen because the scenes are short. After all of the students' scenes have been performed, the guest actors leave and the student directors discuss each scene in a critique session. When critiquing another student's work, classmates can discuss only what they saw, not what was good or bad, not what should've or could've have happened – but what was there, what was revealed and what was made clear. The director cannot explain their choices, they can only listen to the experiences of their peers, what they have seen. It is not long before each director's voice becomes vivid; you can even begin to understand the way they relate to text and actors. You can watch as they lean into the elements of directing – feeling their voice, growing aware of their strengths and weaknesses, and building on that knowledge.

Alongside this process I take time to teach elements of the work of the director by focusing in on the skills (*yes, skills!*) they are developing – like working with actors, dramaturgy, the use of space. But these lessons should be taught in conversation with work and not in terms of dos and don'ts. I also assign in-depth research projects and presentations on directors whose work has made an impact on the field, directors like Bogart, Mnouchkine, Grotowski, etc. It is important when they do this research that they focus on the director's process as opposed to getting bogged down in biography. The students are asked to articulate how the director's work has influenced the field of directing and the theater. By working this way, you plant the seeds of building a practice.

Note to the Queer Auteur. . . *This approach doesn't have to be used only in the classroom. When possible, directors would benefit from using a similar workshop model to engage a new text, project and collaborators. This is the way I work best. Workshopping projects in small increments allows me time to propose a process for working and to work through it on a small scale with fewer stakes. If you can find a way to work like this, it will help you build a practice. Playwrights often develop their script through workshop; this model should be also used by directors while they are engaging a new work.*

Directing Actors

There is a tendency in theater education (and in directing textbooks) to refer to the actor as a position not a person. But actors are real people. They are all coming from somewhere specific; moving through different pathways of training; in fluid relationships to gender, race, their cultural upbringing, history, spirituality, their profession, themselves, their fellow actors, or to you, the director. The complexities of the difference in how, and from where, actors arrive in the room is my favorite thing about directing. It's also what

I love about teaching directing: the actors are a wild card in the room. The director will spend a lot of time figuring out how to respond to what their actors bring or how to get them on the same page or how to coax a lovely performance out of them.

Which leads me to this story. . . For the sake of clarity, I will assume you do not know who Stanley Kowalski is. Stanley Kowalski is the leading male character in Tennessee Williams' play *Streetcar Named Desire*. He is most famously portrayed by Marlon Brando. He is a broody hunk of a man with a hot temper. He's cruel, he's reactionary, and he's terrified by his love for his wife Stella. The fictional character of Stanley Kowalski is a kind of folk hero in New Orleans. There is a "Stella" Shouting Contest at the Tennessee Williams New Orleans Literary Festival every spring where people compete in yelling, "Hey Stella" – a line Brando famously yells from the street up to a second-floor apartment with painfully perfected whiny desperation. It's a contest of who can muster the most defeated plea of a man betrayed by his own hubris.

You might consider. . . going down a wormhole by watching that clip, which can be found on the internet, Marlon Brando yelling "Hey, Stella." Sylvester Stallone uses almost the exact same tone when he, as Rocky, yells "Adrian! Adrian!" Watch that clip, too! The Indigo Girls cover a Dire Straits song called Romeo and Juliet – which totally alters the call to Juliet into a Kowalski-like pleading. You should listen to that, too, to enjoy a lesbian version of that wail.

Now, the story. On the campus where I teach, there is a young person who I can't help but greet with ecstatic enthusiasm. I think my greeting startles him every time. I get so excited to see him because he is my favorite Stanley Kowalski. As the roommate of one of the students in my *Introduction to Directing* class one semester, he was a frequent visitor, coming as an invited actor to perform in all of the scenes she directed. He's like a computer science guy. He's small in stature and walks with an uneven gait. He doesn't "look" the part; he's almost the anti-Stanley Kowalski. I think, for that very reason, my student Sophie had to really work with him and his partner (also an unlikely Blanche, Stella's older sister who comes to live with Stanley and Stella) to learn what made their scene so menacing. Together they had to discover why Stanley and Blanche were so dangerous to one another. They did this through adjustments in vocal energy – by gripping the lines and driving them into each other like twisting a knife. They were constrained and maintained a kind a potential energy, very much like a pendulum at its height, ready to drop. That young man found such a fine balance of ferocity and vulnerability that I believed he was capable of the worst violence against Blanche. Watching him, I felt halted, almost suffocated, by the possibility that at any moment that actual violence could erupt. The work was unnerving, but riveting, and taught all of us in the class so much about the play and also about how Sophie read the play and how Sophie could trust or help her actor to find the character he is playing. In that same class, Zach, an MFA sculpture student, cast his roommates, two soft-spoken, gender-queer folx, as Stanley and Stella. They performed their scene quietly around a tiny little table; Zach asked his actors to rely completely on breath and posture – transforming what is typically performed as a knock-down-drag-out scene into more of a chess match. It was calm and intellectual – conflict rendered acute. When Zach showed the short scene in class, the performers were very close to the audience and they took up almost no space – it felt like watching the scene take place in your lap. I asked him why he made that choice. And he said, "My kitchen is only 6 feet by 6 feet and that's where we rehearsed. I coerced them into acting for me over a dinner I made them. It's just how the scene came out." Zach didn't even try to imagine what he would do if they were actually on a 30 ft by 20 ft stage. He just kept it the way it was in his kitchen. This compactness completely altered where and how tension lurks in the scene. Another student, Greta, a Chinese national studying in the US, found her cast by placing an ad in *Backstage*. Her professional actors stormed around the room slamming doors and kicking chairs. She wasn't quite sure how to work with them because she assumed that they were more expert than her, so she really let them *go to town*! Eventually, in continuing to work with the professional actors, Greta had to rein them in, which taught her a great deal about them. The take-away for the whole class was that you should appreciate and lean in to the uniqueness and individuality of your actors, but also that you cannot ignore the possibility, I might even say the reality, that the very uniqueness and individuality of your actors shapes the play you make. *This is why I am convinced that casting should not be by type – but by instinct, connection, intuition, and possibly even whimsy.*

Casting

Normally, casting is considered to be predictive: you try to predict whether this actor could become this character. But why? What if your choice of actor is NOT predictive, but is treated more like a choice you make in friendship? You could consider who you want to share this experience with instead of choosing who can be this character. Even when considering actors for characters, remember to consider who has the most to give to this character. Actors give something to character; they bring something unpredictable and not scripted. This is the reason that many auteur directors choose to work with the same actors repeatedly. They choose for their relationship and for other shared creative impulses. Their relationships with and trust in the actor are more valuable to the process than surface ideas of character.

Be Familiar with Acting Techniques

Actors enter the rehearsal room with different approaches to acting, different ways of engaging a script, and radically different skills in listening and collaboration. If you are working in a professional environment, then most of the actors you are working with will have had some training and experience. Sometimes the differences among actors' approaches, processes, and techniques can feel to a director like resistances or an imbalance of skills among your cast. Don't allow yourself to make quick (dismissive) judgments. Often what an actor brings into the room is a process that they have established and that they rely on. New collaborators, like new relationships, require an adjustment period for everyone. Take responsibility for each actor by learning their process and techniques, and helping them translate that into the larger rehearsal process.

This kind of care is not always easy, and it may undermine all of your assumptions of the auteur – assumptions that the auteur shapes a work their way and exclusively builds the process and molds the performance from their own brilliance and originality. But even if you have a unique approach to your rehearsals, in order to introduce processes into a room, you must respect and engage the processes that are already there. If you don't do this, then the rehearsal space can quickly become one where some actors thrive and others fail. Actors whose skills and strengths are not seen or nurtured will begin to feel abused by the process and will shut down.

How do we support actors? We might begin by studying acting. This doesn't necessitate going to grad school or spending years in studio schools. Still, it is very possible to learn the major theories, systems and methods, and the vocabularies of the people who will make work with you. I never trained as an actor, but learned this material by teaching acting – by studying and repeating these processes with students. I learned by working with all kinds of actors in my projects. Even the most untrained actor, the DIY actor, has a vocabulary or strategy they rely on.

This all sounds good in theory, but what does it mean to do it? How can you gradually diversify your knowledge of and competency with actor trainings and the various schools of practice?

Fortunately, most methods of actor training have very straightforward genealogies, meaning you can map most methods and systems back to a core vocabulary. The roots of most Western actor training are in Stanislavsky's system and his core strategies for approaching text, actions, and character. Not only did Konstanin Stanislavsky dedicate himself to a deep study of acting, but he created a record of it, wrote books about it, and traveled the world to train others in his system. He sought to understand and articulate the very essence of acting. He wanted to know how actors made choices, how they used their bodies, how they carried their lived experience into their roles. He was able to unpack the work of actors into identifiable tasks. He created a vocabulary for this: actions, activities, beats, objectives, and so on. He eventually left Russia to teach his system in the US and Europe (for political reasons as much as artistic). He also wrote several books explicating and describing the actor's approach, *An Actor Prepares* and *Building a Character*. As he taught, his students across the globe took hold of his ideas and incorporated them into their own methodologies and vocabularies. This is how Stanislavsky's work was transformed by Michael Chekhov, Sanford Meisner, Uta Hagen, Lee Strasberg, and many others. Stanislavsky, however, was less invested in being correct, than he was in understanding what was possible; this is why he supported the work of Meyerhold and Vakhtangov, both experimental directors who worked counter to Stanislavsky's system by exploring theater through shape, time, and biodynamics.

When you consider specific practices like Stanislavsky's system or Anne Bogart's conception of the Nine Viewpoints, you will recognize that these practices are all derived from explorations of human behavior and/or explorations of how the body communicates. These practices all circulate around overlapping foundational ideas that have been re-articulated and tweaked over time. Someone else, usually an auteur director, has taken them up and made them new or their own. This is part of building a practice.

For example, Viewpoints was first introduced as the Six Viewpoints by the choreographer and artist Mary Overlie as a training practice for dancers, performers, and actors. Because Mary Overlie came to the theater as a dancer and a visual artist, she was compelled to introduce models of training that might allow for the hierarchies of the theater to be more flexible. For Overlie, narrative and character were not the most necessary elements to highlight in a show. Anne Bogart (who was Mary's student) translated these ideas into more direct ensemble building and project making (this is the way I see it). Bogart codified the practice of Viewpoints and continued building on the ideas. She applied more teachable constraints by designing a practice of **gridwork** – using an imaginary grid on the floor to guide actors through exploring the nine viewpoints to engage when acting: shape, gesture, architecture, spatial relationship, topography, tempo, duration, and kinesthetic response. We generally refer to this method as Viewpoints because of its outgrowth from the Six Viewpoints, but the two practices are quite different. How you learn them is different, how you use them is different.

Diversify Your Approach

Often in rehearsal, an actor gets hung up in their training, their approach, or their psychological relationship to the text or character. If this happens, change tactics. Stop talking about it. (*If you ask me, the moment when you stop TALKING about it should be often!*). You can often intervene by implementing, or asking actors themselves to make, external choices. There are many problems that can be disrupted or mediated with external choices – choices about breath, rhythm, silence, etc. Sometimes you can just ask the actor to stop thinking or feeling – and then ask them to make a physical adjustment or choice in place of their thought or feeling. You can ask them to do playful or unreal things like, "Could you slowly set the line down on the ground, treating each word like a pebble you are placing next to the last?" You can ask them to take 8 seconds to say their line. You can ask them to whisper and look at the ground – or shout and look at the ground. I mean – you know – just let everyone get some distance, some perspective. These choices can also, of course, be more intentional – they can support something you are imagining rhythmically in the show.

There is a long history of actors learning to inhabit a role physically before they inhabit it emotionally. I like to call this an outside-in approach. This approach stems from Japanese theater traditions like Kabuki and Noh. The kind of training a Kabuki actor receives is sometimes called body-to-body learning because the actor is repeating exact movement or physical scores of another performer – of a master or expert.

You might also consider using scores. We often assume a score is something used to denote music or a dance. But even Stanislavsky describes an actor's physical stage movements as "a score of activities"; this is typically called "blocking" in the theater. Prescribing a score can allow the actor to let the actions and the energy of their body feed their emotions – without the pressure of having to know or determine these things in advance.

Most pedagogies of directing assume that the actor will be the expert on the character and the director will be expert on the play. I don't agree. Actors don't need to be experts, and this "working it out together" is a way the auteur can begin to build unique processes. I think expertise should be elsewhere, it should be in how you engage room, how you listen to an actor or how you find a way to be present to a moment. This kind of expertise allows for discovery and collaboration.

Good directors do not need to be good actors, and they typically aren't – because their minds are often moving in too many directions at once. They rely on a different kind of witnessing than that of the actor. BUT good directors should be competent in teaching or coaching acting. They should focus on their actors' strengths and on balance across the cast. It is possible that on opening night every actor excels because the director has nurtured their strengths – allowing all the actors to see, respect, and respond to difference as a shared power.

THE EDUCATION OF THE DIRECTOR PART TWO: THE CONTINUOUS PRESENT

How Astonishing That We Know This

In her essay, *Experience* Marilynne Robinson reminds us of the depth of knowledge we have about the universe. She also reminds us that knowledge is built from the past, as we have yet to experience the future. "This is remarkable," she writes.[2] We make choices toward future outcomes; and, in doing so, we rely on the experiences that precede the moment of the choice.

You, queer auteur, like all of us, compile experiences both mundane and extraordinary. We collect many of our experiences; we bank them and use them in our work. We also absorb the experience of others through books, through media, through mentorship, and even through intimacy. This is the knowledge that informs our practice.

The abundance of experience and knowledge that precedes us, as theater artists, is truly astonishing. Theater artists have, for centuries, approached their work with a theoretical and practical rigor and have recorded their practices and discoveries. They have passed on their experience by teaching and mentoring. They have penned treatises, developed and recorded methods and systems, expounded on their discoveries through laboratory models of teaching and working. They have written textbooks. They have written manifestos. (*It is probably no longer a secret that this book, these essays, also add up to a kind manifesto.*) What is remarkable is the depth and breadth of all of these accounted-for and recorded experiences. What is complicated is, that as these accounts come to form, they are often organized and codified into systems that attempt to regulate proper and improper practices (good and bad choices) and to construct methodologies to make fixed a whole set of conditions that do not and will not remain still.

Finding Your Own Way through Aristotle's *Poetics*

As a student, I was repeatedly told I must know and be capable of employing Aristotle's elements of dramatic structure if I wanted to be credible as a maker and a teacher. These repeated references to Aristotle's *Poetics* were *always* presented to me as a kind of primer of terminology, as a foundation, as the fundamentals. These were described as the Six Aristotelian Elements of a play: plot, character, theme, language, rhythm, and spectacle.

What are the implications of repeatedly returning to *Poetics* as the life force of drama or, as Aristotle calls it, tragedy? *And* what are the repercussions of using *Poetics* as a manual to codifying play structure? The galvanizing of *Poetics* – as a manual, a guide, a dictionary, a bible – neglects the theoretical and inquisitive call *Poetics* makes. To queer your work or to be an auteur theater director or to unlearn the craft or to simply imagine yourself as an artist practitioner, you must unstick *Poetics*.

One of the events of the research-as-performance project, *I'm Bleeding All Over the Place,* was a panel on the idea of conflict in drama and performance. Experimental theater artists John Jesurun and Kate Valk were among a group of brilliant panelists that included artists Sadie Benning and Moyra Davey and playwright Erin Courtney. About half-way through our conversation, Kate and John broke into a dialogue that delighted the audience and continues to provoke me now. Only recently have I understood that in their complaints against the stasis of theater is *Poetics*! The conversation went like this:

Kate: Well, the theater just remains trapped in the perverse honoring of the playwright.

John: The theater is sort of the last place on earth where this old idea of telling a story..

Kate: (*interjects*) and meaning!

John: (*jumps in*) is still encapsulated in this way we do it – or this way we're supposed to do it.

Kate: This is what it means.

          (*John and Kate are jumping on one another's thoughts.*)

John: All of the other arts, they've gone off into the future.

Kate: Embracing ambiguity. . . it's hard for the theater.

John: It's gotta go: one-two-three-four-five-six-seven-eight.

Kate: Like my mother says 'does it have a beginning, a middle and an end?'[3]

They are talking about Aristotle's *Poetics* and bemoaning the adherence to the codification of the play structure as foundational problem with theater.

That Which Is Consequent

Poetics is a work of aesthetic theory (and this is how it operates in other fields of scholarship). Aristotle's ideas are fodder for much inspiration. Even that core principle of a "beginning, middle and end" can excite. Aristotle says:

> By 'whole' I mean 'with a beginning, a middle and an end'. By 'beginning' [in this context] I mean 'that which is not necessarily the consequent of something else, but has some state or happening naturally consequent on it', by 'end' 'a state that is the necessary or usual consequent of something else, but has itself no such consequent', by 'middle' 'that which is consequent and has consequents.'[4]

If we set aside concerns of ordering, or even story arc, and parse the use of words here: "that which is consequent," that which has "consequents" and consequences.

THIS is exciting! Often, I find myself, especially when teaching acting or directing and looking at something a student has just performed or directed, asking, "How does that operate? What is it doing?" This question can be used in all moments of directing, in every moment in the rehearsal room, inside the making of a play, while talking with the playwright, while talking to a designer, while questioning some desire of a producer or a publicist. What is the **consequent** of a choice? What follows this choice I make now? How will this choice operate? How will it translate into shared experience or meaning? What is its impact?

Does everything boil down to consequences? I hope not. But the questions offered in this middle point of narrative structure, open up a world of possibilities of and for how we come together in a room.

What I find interesting about Aristotle's *Poetics* are all the things that have been left out of contemporary theater education. Immediately after his description of a beginning, a middle and an end, Aristotle discusses amplitude by arguing that objects on stage can neither be too small nor too large. He asks the reader to "imagine, for instance, an animal that is a 1,000 miles long." This creature could not be in a tragedy, he argues, because – even though its size allows for the close inspection necessary to see beauty – its wholeness cannot be taken in at one view (at one time, from one position). The animal that is a 1,000 miles long has an amplitude that exceeds "our view."[5] This argument, which does not translate easily into *craft*, proposes fascinating questions about what is and isn't possible on the stage. What does it mean to zoom in and inspect something from one time and position, but to not have the whole view? Couldn't that also allow for an exciting kind of seeing? Addressing amplitude offers a question that we could use daily in our practice: What is possible on the stage today? Or, sadly, what has been made impossible?

Aristotle discusses the beginning, middle, and end – and the 1,000-mile-long animal – in the very same argument. To him, one seems as essential as the other. How would you receive the rule "you must have a beginning, middle and an end" if it is immediately followed by Aristotle's next rule, "you cannot have an animal that is a 1,000 feet long in your play"? Does this change something?

An insistence on rules and craft and tools of the trade colludes with an insistence on teaching Aristotle as a how-to, rather than as work of play, speculation, and possibility. It is important to point out that, even though it does not seem possible, ever, to have a 1,000-mile animal on the stage, we should consider what the impossible has to do with everything?!?!

Satisfactions

To revisit the diagram that I proposed (in Essay 1) to represent what happens in the space between the production and the audience in section B, imagine that these bubbles represent shared comprehension or a shared experience (Figure 6.1).

Some bubbles are big, some overlap each other, some are contained in one another – while some are almost by themselves on the edge of the dominant bubble. This togetherness and lack of totality or total cohesion is the space of collision.

This drawing is a visual manifestation, a picture fantasy, of what happens during a play over time; but it doesn't account for the changes that occur in all the moments that make up the whole. Theater is a time-based art. To address the event as a whole means to insist on the event as it is hurtling onward, toward its apparent conclusion. Though she is not a director, Gertrude Stein wrote plays and operas that attempt to keep the reader and the audience present in time with her, the writer. In her essay "Plays," Stein refers to this as writing landscapes:

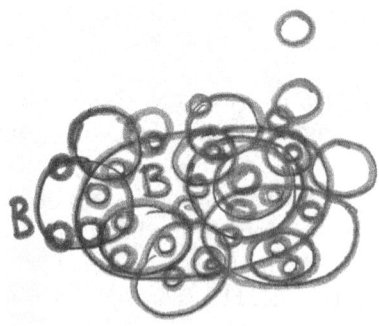

FIGURE 6.1 Sketch by O'Harra of *How the audience receives information.*

I felt that if a play was exactly like a landscape, then there would be no difficulty about the emotion of the person looking on at the play being behind or ahead of the play because the landscape does not have to make acquaintance. You may have to make acquaintance with it, but it does not with you, it is there and so the play being written the relation between you at any time is so exactly that that it is no importance unless you look at it.[6]

Unlike Aristotle's sequential story arc where the middle contains that which has consequent, Stein, working inside of a landscape, moves with and toward moments of satisfaction. She insists that the work come to points of satisfaction. While these moments seem to exist in the moment for the moment, this does not mean that satisfaction cannot add up or accumulate to inform the audience experience. Scholar Daniela Miranda argues that Stein's insistent occupation of the continuous present can be placed in dialogue with contemporary work on queer temporality.[7] (Such work includes the writings of Elizabeth Freeman, Jose Esteban Munoz, and Heather Love, among others.) For instance, Miranda asserts that Stein's work interrupts linearity and the closed signification of normative language structures. Here the queerness of Stein is asserted structurally and linguistically, and both tactics change the temporal relationship between writer and reader or play and spectator.

I want to posit the continuous present as the queer time of theater and to suggest a director's queer time as a component of their work – to develop this space-time and to open up the possibilities for living, acting, and making inside of it.

THE EDUCATION OF THE DIRECTOR PART THREE: TEXTBOOK

Can a Textbook Function in a Continuous Present?

Have you used a directing textbook? When I was a student, I was assigned several directing textbooks. The first was Fundamentals of Play Directing by Dean and Carra, assigned to me for the course Introduction to Directing. This textbook has been widely taught for 80 years. (Take a moment to mull on this - this textbook on directing has circulated for 80 years.) It is a dense and detailed book, organized a bit like a manual and a bit like a syllabus. It is packed with all kinds of specific advice, like this tip found in the sub-section "Embracing and Kissing" inside the section "Handling Certain Emotional Scenes":

> A kiss is often covered and faked for reasons of not smudging make-up, perspiring, or other technical factors. . . .In kissing, the girl, whether standing or sitting, should tilt her head upstage, and the boy his head downstage. This is to be done whether the kiss is actual or covered and faked. . . .[8]

Or this one found in the next sub-section "Sobbing":

> When actors cry, sobbing on their arms, on another's shoulder, in the embrace of another actor, or into a pillow, care should be taken to see that the mouth is not covered-that there is space open in front of it. The forehead and not the face should be laid on the arm, and this will allow the mouth to be protected and the words audible. When the actor cries in the lap of another actor, the upstage side of the face must be in the lap with the front facing out towards the audience.[9]

Reading this again 28 years after I first read it, it makes me rear up and refuse. It makes me want to encourage my actors to smear their make-up, to perspire, and to cry until they can't breathe and have to gasp for air. This textbook advice is outdated and ridiculous, which is hilarious; but it is also suffocating. Suffocation is a common effect produced by the textbook. It reminds me that textbook used as an adjective means performing as instructed, conforming or prescribing to widely held beliefs or practices.[10]

Early in my career, I was frequently told by producers and funders that I needed to "stop reinventing the wheel." This guidance was performed like a scolding. It sounded hopeful and helpful because it promised an easy solution or a clear path toward my aims, but its overall effect was cringy and dismissive. It implied that my choices were naïve, wasteful – perhaps even, failed. Even the most confident person would feel stung by this phrase and the insult behind it.

"Reinventing the wheel" means that there is another way to do the thing you are trying and that you aren't doing it. Check the textbook, you are ignoring the obvious, you are wasting time and energy. It tells you that you don't know *shit*. (*Aside: Shit* is what my friend Ross Gay calls knowledge that people weaponize. He always refers to the "*shit* people say" and "*shit* they do" and "all that *shit*.")

Is this "reinventing the wheel" criticism an attempt to rein in perceived misbehavior? To scold deviancy? Is it a test of how willing I may be to conform when given money, access, and opportunity?

How do we make anything under conditions where *expertise* becomes a frame for control? When I ask *how*, of course, I am asking how is it even possible. I am asking how is it possible to be queer auteurs, when queerness is already recognized as an indulgence in deviancy, a pride in marginality, and a form of resistance?

But in considering the education of the director, I am quite seriously asking *how* do we actually do this? How do we construct queer practices as directors?

In her book *Underdogs,* Heather Love addresses this question as it pertains to the field of Queer studies. In her aptly titled chapter "Doing Being Deviant," Love addresses the possibility and necessity of Queer methods.

> Exploring the history of queer studies confronts us with the fact that the wholesale refusal of normativity does not offer us a viable way forward. Instead, we must make our way with the scholarly tools we have forged, which are, for better or for worse, well suited to analyzing the work that goes into producing reality. We have as our guides in this those scholars from the postwar period, who turned their attention to the business of doing being ordinary, and doing being deviant.[11]

Here Heather is addressing the strategy of queer studies scholars to reject the methods of the social sciences. She acknowledges that these methods often further marginalized their subjects and have rightly been seen as performing a kind of violence on the communities being studied – while, at the same time, these studies recorded and addressed practices of care and communication inside of these so-called deviant communities.

Refusal to perform normatively is a strategy of resistance. But resistance alone does not provide us with the knowledge, community, or cooperation that we need in order to make our projects. Even the most experimental of work has an internal structure or rationale to guide the event. Our field is rich with method. We can interrogate method; we can give attention to the theater artists before us who turned their attention to their own study of *doing* and *being*. We can engage their expertise with openness to these experiences that precede ours. Then we can build upon it, we can transform it, and we can reject it. We can remain in the continuous present.

What I am proposing is that the textbook should not be read as a guide, but as a study or description of a director's experiences. The textbook could be considered a *unique* approach instead of a *universal* approach. Or it can be considered a "study" inside of a field that is truly reliant on and responsive to the practitioners that worked before them. If you refuse the textbook as a guide that can determine how you direct, but you instead read it as description or documentation of studies or a telling of a history, then you can treat it with curiosity. You can be in conversation with it. You can say, "Yes, I do that too!" or "Oh, really? That seems weird. But I can see how sometimes that might be a good choice." or "Wow, I never thought about that." Or, you know, just use shorthand, "OMG!" or "WTF?"

The Making of the Expert

Consider the auteur. Although some may be blessed with deep intuition and good instincts, the auteur does not sprout from the ground as some brilliant spawn of mother earth whose knowledge arrives through magic or destiny. The auteur wrestles with the incongruencies between their own instincts and priorities and those of the experts in their field. They make use of these fissures by choosing what to refuse and what to embrace.

You, vibrant queer auteur, who are already so full of resistance (I didn't need to remind you of that) and also of experience, can be an expert in the field.

When you decide or agree to direct a play or show, you take on a role as the leader; you announce that you will carry this project forward and that you will hold the vision and take responsibility. You will be working with and for many people who believe that the *rules* they learned along the way – are *the way*. You have to be prepared for those encounters.

To be a student of theater (or a leader in the theater), you don't need to rely on a textbook. But you do need to attempt to understand the *shit* that people expect you to know. I'd even say that all the work of this learning, is a learning yourself as a queer auteur. You will also be reminded that this field is built on passion and exploration and that, over the decades, many people before you have followed their curiosity and made exciting proposals, have explored in-depth the work of the actor, and have interrogated the conditions of the theater. You will also bump up against many places where their thinking and doing angers and alarms you. And you will observe a tendency to insist that there is one way to do it right. Immersing yourself in these traditions is necessary, even if it is only the first step toward departing from them. If you have happened upon this essay, then you already know much of this.

I would like for us, together, to devise a kind of working file, an *untextbook* designed specifically for you.

Textbooks

I already told you that Dean and Carra's *Fundamentals of Play Directing* was the first textbook I was assigned. I bought the book for the class; and I still own it and even pick it up from time to time and look through the notes I made in it – the phrases I underlined, the questions I asked in the margins. I was inspired by this book when I was an undergraduate. The other foundational directing texts that I was pointed to as a young director were Francis Hodge's *Play Direction*, Harold Clurman's *On Directing*, and William Ball's *A Sense of Direction*. I absorbed these with a fierce excitement. (A simple online search of directing syllabi will reveal that these texts are still used in some theater classrooms. And most directing classes use a directing textbook. In fact, a colleague of mine proposed that we require all faculty to include one of these texts on their Introduction to Directing syllabi because *"the students need a textbook."*) Another popular and more contemporary directing textbook is Catron and Shattuck's *The Director's Vision*.

I made many notes in those textbooks. I am grateful for those early scribbles because they remind me of the encounter, my enthusiasm, and my "talking back," all of which were necessary for me to gain confidence in my own knowledge. I believe in notes and suggest that you make lots of notes as you study; underline in your books, and write notes in the margin. And be real. Among my notes of earnest admiration, I also wrote things like, "corny," "NOT TRUE!" and lots of "huh?"

The directing textbooks I mentioned voice bold and sometimes wild opinions about the dos and don'ts of directing. They share a great deal of incredibly detailed (*and weird!*) technical instruction. Dean and Carra include sub-sections such as: *"Position after Calling through a door"* and *"Entering and Exiting at Rehearsals."*[12] I mean, um, these titles alone inspire fun fantasies of the play I could be making that requires me to deeply consider the "position after calling through a door." It makes me want to a make a play where everyone is calling through doors – but we only see them in their post-door-calling **positions**.

These textbooks move between helpful advice, insistence on fact and technical how, to illustrations and charts. To demonstrate the landscape of these textbooks, I have pulled excerpts of sections I underlined during my undergraduate studies from *Fundamentals of Play Directing*

Effect of Composition on Audience Emotions
It is a well-known fact that the human is moved emotionally by shapes. . . . Shapes, then, are made up of line, mass, and form. The emotional feeling aroused in the specta-tor by the arrangement of line, mass, and form is known as *mood*.[13]

I had underlined these sentences because, even though I would not call this idea a "well-known fact," there is something that I was and remain drawn to in this consid-eration. I, too, am very interested in how we address the phenomena of our visceral responses to choreography and stage composition and how we explore their possibilities. However, Dean and Carra follow with a kind of bizarre break-down of stage areas – by the mood that is catalyzed by *area* of the stage. Here, 28 years ago, I wrote a large "huh?" in the margin.

Tonal Qualities in Each Area
4. Down left: not so warm as down right: distant intimacy, introspection Scenes Suggested (for Area 4.) Conspiracies, casual love scenes, soliloquies, formal calls, busi-ness matters.[14]

There is something interesting about exploring the geography of the stage, but one should be allowed to be skeptical about carving it up into emotional quadrants. Each staging will have its own logical and emotional resonance, which will depend on all kinds of elements – like time and energy and rhythm. Therefore, these lists or charts counteract the possibility of discovery – by subscribing almost arbitrary rules.

This textbook and others, however, go into extensive detail about every aspect of directing. And, while I find them excessive, I am also inspired by the depth of Dean and Carra's exploration and thinking. There are numerous drawings and diagrams of stage patterns and actors' positionings on the stage. These textbooks are awesome *studies* on how the directors who wrote them made sense of actors' use of the stage. They are also instructive about how the field has been reduced to rules to satisfy the idea that directing is craft.

You are capable of parsing through the material and conceiving that you are in con-versation with these artists (in this case Dean and Carra) who cared deeply about this work. They have considered the actor and the audience and made a system that worked for the room they ran. When I was 19, I had drawn a big circle around the following sec-tion on working with actors. It had an impact on me as a student; and I still agree with much of it.

The Personal Equation

Inspiring the Actors. In the process of bringing a play to performance level, the effectiveness of the director in working with an actor rests as well on the personal equation that goes beyond the talent and the practical know-how of a director. . . .

a Not enforcing but preserving the actor's creative freedom through suggestions rather than declarations.

b Not demanding immediate results, but allowing time for discoveries and growth and understanding. . .

f Talking little, but encouraging questions.

g Reminding the actor to really *see* and *hear*.[15]

Sound familiar? These are concerns I address in essays three and five of this book. **Deep Listening** and **Actors!**.

Textbooks can be practical and commonsense approaches to sharing expertise. They elucidate the complexity of the field and the unpredictability of the rehearsal room. They are full of observations and experiences, and they describe years of encounters with the dilemmas we face as directors. But, as they further attempt to translate particular observations and experiences into generalized rules, they remind me of my consternation with teaching directing.

Ask yourself. When do you resist guidance and when do you accept offers from others? How do you work in close collaboration with theater artists who have grounded themselves in expert knowledge, in craft? How do you make a rehearsal room that allows for a process and practice that can play loose and easy with the rules, but can also utilize them?

Alexander Dean died in 1939, the same year as Konstanin Stanislavsky. Lawrence Carra gathered Dean's lessons and incorporated them into book form, first published in 1941. This textbook is an in-depth articulation of a teaching and a directing practice, one that might be perfect for Noël Coward and Neil Simon plays and even for G.B. Shaw. The book describes a process that promotes a tight, resistance-free approach in which actors travel in clear paths and sit upright in their chairs, do stage business, speak in clear, articulated voices, and perform tidy kisses! Dean and Carra's experience shows us something about choices that have worked but also lets us, in an encounter with theirs, learn about the choices we make, we will make, and those we want to make. It also shows us the structure within which directing normatively operates – one that incorporates systems and theories that have developed over time. It demonstrates how you might translate your own practice (or your own experience).

You can do this – you can articulate your practice. At the very least, you can put your work into conversation with the experience that is already out there. Not necessarily for others, but for yourself. You can do this regularly, record and grow your practice, while also allowing for your ideas to change as you change and as the world around you evolves.

Notes

1 During my time at Mt. Holyoke College, the school revised its admission policies. They now accept "female, transgender and non-binary" applicants.

2 Marilynne Robinson, "Experience," in *The Givenness of Things* (New York: Picador, 2016), 226.
3 Brooke O'Harra, Panel Conversation: A Conversation on a Few Topics Relevant to Actors, Playwrights, Directors, and Artists, Including Gender, the Everyday, and the Extraordinary Problem of "Conflict Removed" (New Museum, New York, 2014).
4 Margaret Hubbard, "Aristotle," in Ancient Literary Criticism edited by Donald Andrew Russell and Michael Winterbottom (Oxford: Clarendon Press, 1972), 100.
5 Ibid., 111.
6 Gertrude Stein, "Plays," in *Look at me Now and Here I Am: Writing and Lectures 1911–1945* edited by Patricia Meyerowitz (London and Chester Springs: Peter Owen Publishers, 2004), 75.
7 Daniela Miranda, *The Queer Temporality of Gertrude Stein's Continuous Present* (Köln: Gender Forum, Issue 54, 2015), 20–32. Miranda marks the work of Elizabeth Freeman, Jack Halberstam, Jose Esteban Munoz and I can include Heather Love as well.
8 Alexander Dean and Lawrence Carra, *Fundamentals of Play Directing* (Holt, Rinehart and Winston, Inc, 5th Edition, 1965), 56.
9 Ibid.
10 Textbook *adj.* (2022) Google Dictionary from Oxford Languages. Retrieved from https://www.google.com/search?client=safari&rls=en&q=definition+of+textbook&ie=UTF-8&oe=UTF-8
11 Heather Love, *Underdogs* (Chicago and London: University of Chicago Press, 2021), 160.
12 Alexander Dean and Lawrence Carra, *Fundamentals of Play Directing* (Holt, Rinehart and Winston, Inc, 5th Edition, 1965), 49.
13 Ibid., 119.
14 Ibid., 135.
15 Ibid., 265–266.

Your UNTEXTBOOK

This companion piece to the essays *The Education of the Director* is designed to encourage you to continue to grow your practice. This section is organized as a kind of workbook with prompts, reading recommendations, and some descriptions of process. It could be used by directors, students, instructors, and any of you at any stage in your work. The organization is a bit piecemeal because I am assuming that you will navigate through your own interests and engage at your own pace. Sequence it as you please. Skip around. Return to it. Refuse it. Rewrite it. Make it into something that can suit you. What I am saying is – do with it as you please. I wrote this for you.

DOI: 10.4324/9781003253402-7

WHAT THE DIRECTOR DOES

What Does a Director Do?

Take some time to describe the role of the director as you understand it <u>right now</u>. Write down everything you know about what the director does. Describe the process and the rehearsal room. Describe how the director should approach texts, actors, design and designers, and rehearsals. *I bet you will be surprised by this process, because I have a feeling that you already know a lot!*

Do this now and then do it each time you are about to start a new project. You will find that your priorities and thinking change. Each new project asks that you engage it as the artist you are now, in the circumstances and conditions that you are living in and working in now, and with the people who you are collaborating with now. These always changing circumstances should affect how you approach your practice on each new project. By writing a fresh version of this document, you are also acknowledging that directing is a practice and that your approach can and will change.

BE AN ACTING COACH

It is your job to support each actor's best work. To access an actor's strengths, you have to know how to address their process. You should strive to develop the ability to translate, for yourself, the actor's process and training. This will allow you to give specific, clear direction and to avoid addressing their choices through negation like "don't do this." Most likely the actors have built practices from a variety of methods and have honed them into a system that works best for them. Building a common language or a shared vocabulary is very doable as long as you make the effort to meet each actor where they are. From here, you can draw your cast toward shared vocabularies.

It is possible (*and I believe it is necessary*) to become quite adept and agile at translating across systems/training methods, which can allow you to work succinctly and thoughtfully in the rehearsal room.

You have been granted access by many great artists who precede you to use their methods and systems. You have the permission to draw on this body of work. But, in return, you should give permission to the actors to use the systems and training that they know and depend on. Work together. Build trust.

Prompt

Study the Books

There are numerous books on actor training. Explore them. Try the exercises. Study the terminology. I have found that the compilations that distill practices are a useful way to start as well as a useful reference.

Resources

The two books that I rely on are as follow *Training of the American Actor* and *Actor Training*

Training of the American Actor *edited by Arthur Bartow*

This compilation of essays on actor training does an incredible job of distilling the work of American theater artists whose work remains at the base of actor training in U.S. acting programs. The essays are written by theater professionals who continue to teach their methodologies. The chapters are succinct; they highlight important terminology and recreate useful practical exercises. The book is designed so that you can cover a large scope of training very quickly.

Barlow has a great chapter on *Uta Hagen's Technique* and another useful one on *Mary Overlie's Six Viewpoints*. I teach these two chapters regularly. I recommend you do the exercises – or ask your actors to do the exercises.

Training for the American Actor also has chapters on several of the major theorists of acting technique, including Lee Strasberg, Stella Adler, Michael Chekov, Stephen Wangh, and Robert Bella.

Actor Training *edited by Alison Hodge*

This book also covers and distills actor training that we have inherited from Western and Eastern European countries as well as some methods established by American directors. I often have my Introduction to Directing and Introduction to Acting students read a chapter in this book called *Stanislavsky's System: Pathways for the Actor* by Sharon Marie Carnicke. Carnicke is an acting teacher who has combined Stanislavsky's biography with a short concise breakdown of his system; exercises are included. She does an excellent job of defining his terms. This chapter is a succinct and user-friendly summary of Stanislavsky's history and his system for beginning actors. Carnicke does a great job of explaining his terms and she makes clear the differences between terms that might seem indistinguishable like an action and activity (*I find this helpful*). She introduces Stanislavsky's use of "score," as in "scoring" both your actions and activities. She describes beats and how they are used.

This book also has chapters on: Stella Adler, Eugenio Barba, Augusto Boal, Anne Bogart, Bertolt Brecht, Peter Brook, Michael Chekhov, Joseph Chaikin, Jacques Copeau, Philippe Gaulier, Jerzy Grotowski, Maria Knebel, Jacques Lecoq, Joan Littlewood, Sanford Meisner, Vsevolod Meyerhold, Ariane Mnouchkine, Monika Pagneux, Michel Saint-Denis, Włodzimierz Staniewski, and Lee Strasberg.

Dig deeper. Anthologies are useful because they compile the deep knowledge of people who have been teaching these techniques and systems for decades, they distill the vocabulary and exercises into a concise first encounter, but you could and should go to the source and read the full books written by the folks whose life work is being summarized like: Stanislavsky, Uta Hagen, Meyerhold, Bogart, Zeami, Suzuki, etc. These artists all have books of their own that can expose you to their lives in the field and the very personal investments and exploration that led to the training and the language we use in the rehearsal room today.

Prompt

Terms

Make a list of all the terms related to acting that you come across.
Example – Actions, activities, beats, objectives, score, movement, flower, breath.
Add to it whenever new terms arise. Rewrite and reorder it. This should be active and generative – and likely repetitive.

Prompt

Terms in Relation

On a separate page or in another section of your notebook place these terms in relation or in groups that are similar (but not exactly the same). Indicate words that are sometimes used interchangeably. There doesn't have to be a hierarchy. Maybe they are in clumps or boxes.

Some of mine are:
> objective – wants – throughline
> Actions – verbs

Term Chains

On another page, write definitions or descriptions of the words. You should feel free to use other terms in your definitions. This helps you to see how they are interchanged and connected.

This is how I might do this – An **activity** is something an actor physically does on the stage. A **score of activities** is a chain of **activities** that the actor uses on the stage. We also call this **blocking**. This is not the same as an **action.** But we often use an **activity** to show or mark a **beat change** which can be demarcate a change in **action**.

OR

An **action** is what the character is **doing** to another character on the stage. For example, an action might be to seduce the other character. In this case seduce would be the **action.** This is also referred to as a **verb.** When you write down all of the actions of a character, this is called a **score of actions**. Creating a **score of actions** is similar or even the same as doing **verb work.** These are the small **objectives** that propel a scene. Other people call **objectives "wants,"** but an **action** and a **want** are not the same, it is the characters **want** or **objective** that fuels their **actions.** When a character gets what they **want** (or doesn't) but they change their **action**, this is when there is a **beat change**.

By doing this exercise you start to see how these terms are all connected and how they are often substituted for each other, but they are all hovering around the same approaches. Don't get bogged down by how tricky or confusing this can get. Instead, treat it like a puzzle. Perhaps you could find some play or pleasure in the slipperiness or these terms.

Advanced Term Chains

I find doing term chains to be a fun activity. Once you are comfortable with it, you can extend this work to something like Zeami's treaties on Noh drama or Anne Bogart's Viewpoints. You can consider how terms like Flower and Skin and Bone (from Zeami) relate to terminology we use to describe embodiment. You can consider where physical approaches to acting relate to mental approaches.

USING QUESTIONS

The kind of knowledge building that I am encouraging takes time. (*It took me decades!*) You can never be fully prepared to work with every actor who enters the room. I find that the best **short cut** to understanding the actor's practice is through asking questions.

Learn how to alter an impulse from telling someone what to do, to asking them questions? Questions allow for actors to find their own way toward understanding their choices and making other choices. Questions in the rehearsal room encourage actors to listen to each other. Questions help you to learn the actors' approach and process.

Simple and useful questions would be:

Where will you start?

Why do you think your character is doing that?

What does your character want right now?

Why did you move there? Could you move somewhere else?

What is your relationship to that piece of furniture? (*That one sounds stupid, but it is not.*)

How can your character get that thing they want from that that character?

How can you change the feeling in this room?

What do you need?

What are you hearing?

What happens if you change your energy or tempo? What are all the possible tempos you could use?

What are you doing with your breath?

What other ways can you breathe in this moment?

Where do you want to direct your gaze? And what happens when you look there?

Prompt

What Are <u>Your</u> Questions?

Write down questions that you use or that come to mind as you read this list. If you have things you regularly say to actors in rehearsal that are not questions, see if you can change them into questions. Keep a running list in your notebook. Go back and refresh.

You might have recognized that many of my questions were about what the actor was physically doing. I find it helpful to move back and forth between a kind of scene study/ actions and wants approach to acting and an outside-in approach. And depending on the project I will lean in more toward one or the other. But I find moving in between these approaches creates some space, keeps choices open longer and allows for new feelings and ideas to slip in. You may also use other tools of the theater, like employing strategies as simple as giving the actor strict blocking or creating concrete physical prompts or giving directions to push a scene outside of intellectual or emotional considerations. You may rely heavily on dramaturgy. This depends on what you need to achieve and how you feel comfortable working.

SHARE LEADERSHIP WHEN IT IS POSSIBLE

The use of questions allows for people to assert their opinions and engage with you in making choices. You are setting up a scenario where someone else might have better answers than you. Good. In rehearsal you will find that some people in the room are better at some things than you are. When those people surface in the room, put them in charge of those things. Making space for shared responsibility is hugely productive.

For example, when I was rehearsing *Drum of the Waves of Horikawa* we created scores from footage of hard core and punk rock concerts. These moves were kind of wild and arbitrary, they were not choreographed. However, we wanted to learn them exactly, as a choreography. One actor in our company, Mike Mikos, was particularly skilled at translating the moves from the screen to the body. He was great at coaching the other actors in learning these moves. So, we made him dance captain. By doing this – everyone felt better cared for. He felt seen and respected and the others felt in good hands, and I could focus on other important details.

Typically, the actors' depth and breadth of skill is much greater than my own. So, when we are doing something that requires a deep understanding of craft – like singing or dancing. I like to find someone in the cast who will lead the group in training and development. Doing this isn't taking advantage, it is acknowledging that we are a community and can pass on and share skills with care and respect.

Prompt

Acknowledge Your Methods

Take a moment to write down the approaches you use with actors. Write as many approaches as you can remember. *Consider your approach. Have you articulated this in writing before?*

KNOW YOUR ROOM

Be ready for rehearsal. One of the most important rooms you will occupy as a director is the rehearsal, room. There is not one way to start a rehearsal nor is there one way to rehearse a show. How you start and how you approach a text is dependent on the project and on your own practice. Some people always use the same process. For example, they may always start with table work or with improvisation or with an introduction to the project and team. Some directors may always do warm-ups at the beginning of a rehearsal. Directors often do this because they are repeating something that they experienced as an actor – or because they think that is what the actors expect of them. But you don't necessarily need to start each process or each day the same. Maybe you are building a show that demands the actors be very large and exuberant. In that case, you may just start by dancing or exploring techniques for building a physical vocabulary. Perhaps you are working on a difficult text like Toshiki Okada's *Enjoy*. This play has no full-stops and moves from first person to third person inside of lines; characters move across actors. If you are working on a play like this, then you may spend several days sitting at a table reading through the script and working together to understand the internal logic of the text with your actors.

Prompt

Running Rehearsals

Take a moment to write down how you engage your actors. Write as many things as you can remember about how you run rehearsals. What are your strengths? What might your actors do better than you? Consider your approach to the rehearsal room. Have you articulated how you run rehearsal writing before?

Time – The time you have in the room together is invaluable. Don't squander it. Be smart about time. This means be prepared for rehearsal. Have a plan in advance – and be careful to avoid activities that use time but may not benefit the process.

Talking – Don't get bogged down with a lot of talking at your team. You can't talk a play into being great. If you want to share research or ideas, then make time for it; but balance that time by having people actively working and engaging with the project. Talking about something isn't the same as doing it.

Warm-ups – Address warm-ups on the first day. Learn how your actors use warm-ups and what they need to do at the top of rehearsal to be ready and focused. Don't do warm-ups just to do them. Before doing an exercise, be clear what the purpose is and how it will help your actors that day in that rehearsal. There are a lot of good warm-ups for voice, for learning how to respond to the space, for building your ability to react in real time to each other, etc. But you should choose these based on what you plan to be doing that day. Don't just do warm-ups because that is how you have been taught to start rehearsal – and don't do arbitrary warm-ups. How you start matters. That sets the tone for the day. Have a plan for how to start each rehearsal. Build a clear and dependable plan for warm-ups. When necessary, let the actors help be responsible for them. Warm-ups are different than exercises. Some actors prefer to do their own warm-ups. Let that happen.

Keep a Warm-up Archive

Write out the **warm-ups** that you do. If the warm-up doesn't have a name, give it one. Describe how the warm-up is done and why you would do it. I also like to record where I learned it. I also made many of my own exercises.

Example –

The Vowel-Tree – This is a combination movement and voice warm up. The Vowel Tree Exercise enables us to practice making sounds with our voice and exploring the vowels in our entire vocal range from low to high. The sounds are accompanied by various moves in your body. This is an exercise that Kristen Linklater developed for acting Shakespeare. There are videos of it online.

I do this exercise because it opens the actors' vocal range, it also loosens the actors up. I like to do it twice through and then assign actors to do a free-style version – bouncing around the sounds – the other actors follow. This also introduces a kind of listening and repeating and play. I like for actors to be comfortable with these kinds of leading/following explorations.

I learned this in graduate school in an Acting Shakespeare class.

Speaking on your voice – This exercise must follow breathing exercises. The actors should be ready to breathe deeply via the diaphragm and should have opened their voice. Each actor takes two lines that they speak in the show. I stand as far away as possible and they line up in a line and speak the line to me as clearly and fully as they can. They must not yell, and they must recognize when they have to take a breath.

This exercise reminds them what it feels like to project on the stage. It is a way to set that feeling in the bodies before the house opens. I do this exercise once we are in the theater and on show nights. It is a nice way for the actor to remind their body what you expect of it.

It is more useful for inexperienced performers, but it is good for everyone to check-in with their voice on the stage before a show – to make sure they have reminded themselves how much air they need behind the words in order to be heard. This is becoming more important because the use of microphones is becoming more widespread – so actors are not always performing with the same level of vocal projection from show to show.

This is an exercise that I created for the moment when a cast moves from the rehearsal room onto the stage.

EXPERIENCES WITH BOOKS

When I was a young director, I was given great advice on dramaturgy. The advice was that I should do all the dramaturgical work in advance; I should learn what I could about the text, its history, its context, its style or genre and so on. Then I was told to set the research to the side before I entered the rehearsal room. The idea is that if you do the preparatory work, then you can trust that you have access to that information when necessary. But by setting it aside, you aren't trying to include everything you learned – you only draw from the knowledge that is most relevant. This has worked for me.

Prompt

Become a Dramaturg of Directing . . . build a reference list of books that expose you to the experience and knowledge of directors, artists, scholars and activists who came before you.

Resources

I choose to organize these texts into four categories:

Directing textbooks – Textbooks typically demonstrate a how-to approach. They break down directing into categories and then give detailed instruction on each step or element of the directing process. Some have sections that function like an instruction manual.

Directors' books on approach and theory -- These texts are authored by directors who have made a significant contribution to the field and who have spent their career exploring approaches to directing, acting and the theater. In these texts the directors break down their discoveries and beliefs and they discuss their work or approaches. They often contextualize their practice and some share exercises and methods. These contributions are invaluable to our field and knowing about them has been essential to my work, even when I encounter them after I have already struggled through similar questions on my own. The most available, familiar and sited of these texts are.

Antonin Artaud – *The Theater and its Double*
Anne Bogart – *The Viewpoints Book* and *A Director Prepares*
Bertolt Brecht – *Brecht on Theater*
Peter Brook – *The Empty Space*
Joseph Chaikin – *The Presence of the Actor*
Jerzy Grotowski – *Towards a Poor Theatre*
Uta Hagen – *Respect for Acting* and *A Challenge for the Actor* (Hagen was an actor but I am
    including her book. Hagen found that actors were misreading *Respect for the Actor* so as a
    corrective she wrote *A Challenge for the Actor* in hopes of clarifying some misconceptions
    about her process.)
Tadashi Suzuki – *The Way of Acting*
Zeami – *On the Art Of Noh Drama*

Books that explicate, describe or summarize the work of important directors – These texts are written by artists, teachers and scholars who have worked with or studied auteur directors. They have taken it upon themselves to break down a director's work into easily teachable lessons or usable strategies. They have condensed the work of the director into key points. These books/chapters/essays do a nice job of articulating the impact that the director has had on the field and how their contributions have been incorporated into rehearsal rooms and processes.

These books matter because they cover a more diverse selection of directors like: Ariane Mnouchkine, Joan Littlewood, Moisés Kaufman, George C. Wolfe.

Books that don't have anything to do with directing but have taught you how to direct, how to read a play or how to be with people in a room.

This track is very individual and will morph and change as the world changes. It may include queer theory and black studies or practical essays on living and politics. You may spend a lot of time with scholars who engage performance and politics like José Esteban Muñoz, Fred Moten, Sara Ahmed, Heather Love, or artists whose formal choices are bound in up in their research, aesthetics and politics like Ralph Lemon, Emily Johnson, Sadie Benning and Pope L. You may also rely on archives as a window into the work of culture, politics and movements that informed this moment. *(I highly recommend you visit a queer archive in person to fully understand the wonder of the archive.)*

This work of engaging with the experience of others, this unique kind of dramaturgy, draws upon two important and possibly conflicting ideas: one is that directing has a rich history and many incredible directors have generously shared with you what they have learned about the art; the other is that there is no correct way to do directing. Through building a practice you are addressing these ideas simultaneously; you are using the structures and systems that are in place and using your experience and shared experience to make them your own.

Some additional advice . . . Accounting for all of the materials in these books is an impossible task. Don't let that get you down. Work at your own pace and trust your own path. Where you could push yourself is in constructing a frame or map of the knowledge you encounter, find a way to mark or record how ideas land for you, how they inspire you and teach you. Take the time to write down, copy or collect the ideas that are most important for you.

I read many of the books (that I recommended) by directors over a two-year period because they were shelved in the English language section of my local library in Narita, Japan. It was because Japanese translations of these texts were not readily available that I was even able to access these books at important moment in my life. I was living in some isolation, so I could make a deep dive. And I kept chapter by chapter notes (when I was age 22). I still reference them; I wrote these notes *as if I were in conversation with the text. For example, while reading Peter Brook's Empty Space* I wrote these notes (Figure 7.1).

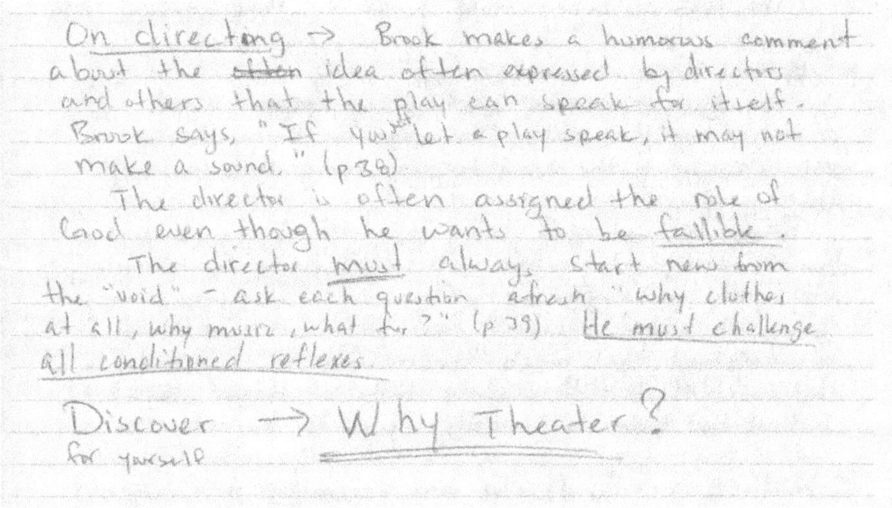

On directing → Brook makes a humorous comment about the ~~often~~ idea often expressed by directors and others that the play can speak for itself. Brook says, "If you let a play speak, it may not make a sound." (p.38)
The director is often assigned the role of God even though he wants to be fallible.
The director must always start new from the "void" – ask each question afresh "why clothes at all, why music, what for?" (p 39). He must challenge all conditioned reflexes.

Discover → Why Theater?
for yourself

FIGURE 7.1 Image from O'Harra journals written in 1996, Narita, Chiba, Japan.

You can also force these directors in conversation with each other. Analyze what you see from one director through the perspective of another. In that same notebook, I copied a passage from the Empty Space pages 61–62 and then followed with this observation.

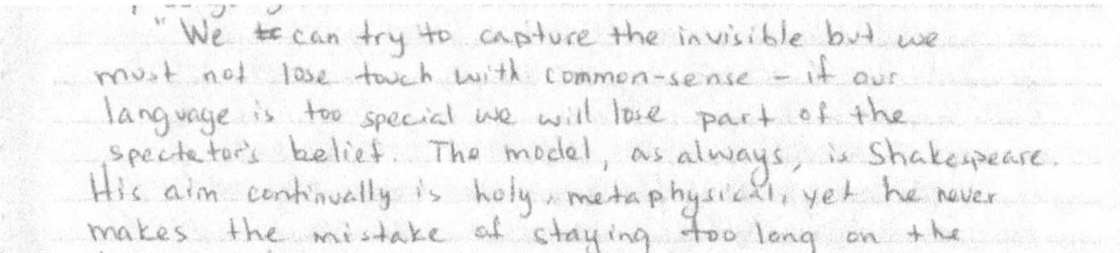

"We ~~to~~ can try to capture the invisible but we must not lose touch with common-sense – if our language is too special we will lose part of the spectator's belief. The model, as always, is Shakespeare. His aim continually is holy, metaphysical, yet he never makes the mistake of staying too long on the highest plane. He knew how hard it is for us to keep company with the absolute – so he continually bumps us down to earth. ... We have to accept that we can never see all of the invisible. So after straining towards it, we have to face defeat, drop down to earth, then start up again." (61-2)
This is a very wise observation – and puts me in my place – a nice reminder that we cannot push and push our audience – we must allow them times to lay low in the realm of the familiar. I think that, perhaps, the reason LeCompte and Foreman and the like get lost on the audience is because they do not take this into consideration. They think that they must place the audience on a plain of constant accelerated thoughts and image – they bring the audience deep and deep them deep – eventually they have to come up for air, rest their mind, reunite with the familiar – here they step out of the performance – and the performance isn't ready to guide them back in.

FIGURE 7.2 Image from O'Harra journals written in 1996, Narita, Chiba, Japan.

I share these notes because I wrote them when I was 22 and I can't imagine how I could have conceived that I knew what I was talking about. I mean – what was I talking about? It doesn't matter, because what I was doing was working. I was engaging the field as if I were already a professional director. I was inserting myself into the conversation and was making sense of all of these texts as ideas and proposals – not rules. And, most importantly, I am urging you to do something similar. I am urging you to become an *expert* by inserting yourself into this centuries-in-the-making conversation about directing. I am suggesting that as an expert you need not be correct, that you needn't imitate or copy these practices but that you can respond to them and that you learn from them. That this experience that has been recorded for you with such care and passion, can be drawn into your own experience. And beginning now, you, too, like these folks before you, can articulate record your own practice.

ALL PLAYS ARE NOT ALIKE

Plays are engagements.

Most theater textbooks describe directing as a more or less coherent process that can be applied in most, if not all, spaces, at most, if not all, historic moments, with most, if not all, plays. But plays push and change the process of directing. Plays are not all the same and they often demand something distinct in each step of the process.

A show is built over time through rehearsal. Prior to rehearsals you make choices about who is in the room with you, you cast the project and you build a team of collaborators-- these are designers, stage management and possibly a writer or writers. If the script you are working with is finished and the playwright is not present for the rehearsal process, they may still be in the room with you in spirit or they may be accessible for questions or conversation. But even a playwright is not the play – the play is its own presence in the room.

Most frequently a play is written or partially written before you began rehearsals. How you and the play come together is dependent on a variety of circumstance and choices. But regardless of the circumstances that bring you together, you are now in a relationship with that play. And that is a relationship you bring into the rehearsal room and nurture with your collaborators. To prepare yourself for that work you need to know plays.

Prompt

Make a Reading List

Read plays and read materials about plays and authors. Make a list of plays you want to read and work your way through that list, adding new ones whenever they come to you. You will make your own logic and order for your reading, you will make your own record, you will keep your own time.

Resources

If I were asked to make a kind of general list today of what I would recommend to a director that list might look like this.

Greek Tragedies and Comedies

You have likely heard of Sophocles, Euripides and Aristophanes. And you may even know the story of Dionysis and Oedipus and Medea. But you should be familiar with the structure and practice of this early theater. Greek tragedy and comedy constitute one origin of theater as we know it. And many playwrights have translated and reimagined these narratives, these characters and the structural elements of these plays. Greek drama seeps into the theater everywhere. So . . . it helps to be familiar with the texts and authors of Greek drama. You don't need to sit down and read them all, but I would suggest knowing what they are and who wrote them and who is making plays based on them. Return to the Greeks from time to time for a check in.

Shakespeare

It will be difficult to navigate the field of theater without some exposure to Shakespeare. Read some history plays, comedies and tragedies. Don't just see productions. Read parts aloud from time to time. I also think a familiarity with voice coaches who teach Shakespeare is incredibly helpful – people like Kristen Linklater or Cecily Berry who can address how the sound, meter and punctuation of the plays produce story and character.

Also, read Shakespeare's contemporaries, Ben Jonson (*Volpone, or the Fox*) and Christopher Marlow (*Tamburlaine*)

Read a William Wycherley play (*The Country Wife*), Moliere, Aphra Behn, and Richard Brinsley Sheridan (*School for Scandal*).

Take your time with the modernists

Strindberg

Shaw – You might also read Shaw's essay *Ibsenism*.

O'Neal

Ibsen – If you read *Hedda Gabler* you may find pleasure in pairing that with Fornes' *Summer at Gossensass*.

Note on Ibsen, Strindberg, and O'Neal: Ibsen was considered the "father of realism" and all three worked in realism but all three also took a surrealist turn. You may want to consider that when you read them. For example, you may want to read *Hedda Gabler* and then *Peer Gynt*, or with Strindberg *Miss Julie* and then *Ghost Sonata*, O'Neal's *The Iceman Cometh* and *Hairy Ape*.

Symbolism

Read Chekhov – read about Chekhov and read both a long play and some of his short plays. (I will confess here that *The Cherry Orchard* is one of my favorite plays.)
Amari Baraka (*Dutchman*) (also could be Avant Garde)

American Realism (with some symbolism)

Read Tennessee Williams (also in Queer section)
Read August Wilson (also considered part of the Black Arts Movement)
Eugene O'Neal (also in Modernism)

Absurdism

Read a play by Ionesco and Pinter and several by Beckett

The Avant-Garde

You must read the mother of the avant-garde Maria Irene Fornes
Suzan-Lori Parks (read 3 play her at least) definitely read *The Death of the Last Black Man in the Whole Entire World* (another of my favorite plays)
Adrienne Kennedy - definitely read *A Movie Star has to Star in Black and White*

Feminists

Jane Bowles (*My Sisters Hand in Mine* and other writings)
Susan Glaspell's (*Trifles*)
Caryl Churchill

Know your queer writers

Oscar Wilde
Gertrude Stein (pair her plays with her essay *Plays*. Learn about landscape theater.)
You must read Maria Irene Fornes (read at least 4 of her plays, but definitely *Mud*, *Fefu and Her Friends* and at least 1 from *Letters to Cuba*)
Genet (read 2 – definitely *The Maids*)
Tennessee Williams (definitely *Streetcar Named Desire*)
Rainer Werner Fassbinder (*The Bitter Tears of Petra von Kant*)
Tony Kushner (*Angels in America* both parts)
Five Lesbian Brothers
Split Britches
Lisa Kron
Madeleine George (*Precious Little* is again a favorite)
Paula Vogel
Jeremy O. Harris
Agnes Borinsky
Haruna Lee
Kristen Kosmas
Don't waste time on rabid misogynists like David Mamet.

Contemporary (2000s – onward)

This list could go on and on (and will go on and on) and nobody expects you to know all of these writers' works so, please, create your own list of contemporary playwrights. These are contemporary playwrights that I regularly teach because they teach me about form, language, voice, and bodies on stage.
Erin Courtney
Quiara Alegría Hudes
Heidi Schreck

Celine Song
Branden Jacobs-Jenkins
Jackie Sibblies Drury
Will Eno (*Tragedy a Tragedy*)
Thomas Bradshaw
Robert O'Hara
Amina Henry (*Bully*)
Lynn Nottage
Karinne Keithly Syers
Tina Satter
Young Jean Lee
Toshiki Okada (*Enjoy*) writes in Japanese but has works in translation by Aya Ogawa

Don't expect to get through this reading list quickly. As you chip away at it you should also keep adding to it and diverging from it. You might be lucky enough to cover some this material in classes or on projects, but just keep moving through your list, reminding yourself to talk to and listen to the text. I can never really comprehend all the complexities of a play until I start to hear and see it in the rehearsal room. So I think of these first encounters as, just that – a reading – making a pass or two over the text to get a loose sense of what it is doing and how it could operate, or just to enjoy the language or the story.

Prompt

Make a Record of Your Experience Reading

Once you have a list, or some portion of a list, then work through your list with curiosity. Take stock of how you respond to the text as you move through it. Perhaps you can do this by recording notes after you have read the play. Consider these questions. Do you respond to narrative, character, structure, or something else? What gives the play heat for you? What about this playwright excites, surprises or seduces you? Can you read the script in a way that allows you to step back from story and look at the form of the work, the conceits, the patterns? Don't fixate on scholarly practices like close readings, avoid the pitfalls of knowing what something is. My friend the playwright and artist Kristen Kosmas told me that "all readings are misreadings." Learn yourself as a reader and a misreader. Be fluid and be impulsive with your responses. There is no great urgency to really know the work or be an expert, you can do that if and when it becomes necessary, with others in a rehearsal room.

BE YOUR OWN DRAMATURG

Getting Intimate with a Play

A first read of a play could be like a first date or a casual introduction. You should simply allow for your first reactions to seep in. But if you're going to direct a play, you should get to know it. Be your own dramaturg. (Or work intimately with a dramaturg who is your collaborator and not the voice of an institution.) Dramaturgy is all the research that you engage to better understand the terms and world of the script you are working with. I break down my dramaturgical research into genre, the author, the historical era/politics/place, and (when possible) the production history of the play itself.

Dramaturgy by Category

Genre or Form

I have categorized some of the plays by genre or categories like Surrealist or Avant Garde. But what does that mean? Or why does it matter? Theater like visual art has been influenced by artistic movements which were often derived in response to the politics and culture of that moment. These formal interventions into classical ideas of narrative give us new ways to tell story and new operations for engaging an audience. Even a most basic understanding of these movements can change the way you read a play.

Author

There is a great deal of information circulating about playwrights like Shakespeare, Ibsen, Chekhov, O'Neal; there is so much so that everyone behaves like an arm chair expert – scholars and audiences alike. But what do you know about the playwright? What is their world view or their formal concerns? What does their body of work look like and did it change over time? Who did they know, what other artists and writers were they in conversation with and what were their politics? These same questions can be applied to contemporary writers. The total work of a playwright is very telling. My awareness of the small (or big) things happening in a script is often informed by my understanding of a writer and their larger body of work. See the writer as someone in a broader conversation than this one play, with both the field and the form of theater. Engage that conversation with them.

History, Politics and Place or the Archival World of the Play

This research has the most branches of exploration and will vary based on the script you are working with. Many texts are written in response to specific historical and political moments. The time, people, the story – these are often specific. There is so much to discover about the world of a play by digging deeper into the time, place, people that the text addresses. A play has a huge context in which it sits. It is so much fun working backwards from the script and learning about the larger context of the setting and cultural moment.

Production History

Not all plays hang around for decades, but many do. And when that happens a play has its own production history. There are reviews and descriptions of productions and there may be a famous production or movies of the play. This history becomes part of the event of your production – whether or not you want it there – it exists as a kind of shadow or trace. Again, your production is in conversation with those productions whether or not you actively choose to engage that conversation. For this reason, I always suggest that you don't shy away from or ignore the records of past performances. You might be worried about unwanted influence or other issues that arise from knowing about previous productions. But I think all this information is helpful, because I cannot express enough how important it is that you do not isolate yourself. Be open and curious (I have said this before) about the entire frame of the event of your play.

INDEX

Note: *Italic* page numbers refer to figures.

acting 4, 9, 23, 63–69, 94, 95; art and community 74; bad 29–30, 45, 46; coaching 79, 92; real people 61; Stanislavsky's system 39, 51; teaching 79, 81; techniques 77–79
An Actor Prepares (Stanislavsky) 51
Actor Training (Hodge) 92–93
Akerman, Chantal 3
Andres, Jo 29
Angeles, Moe 29, 30, 68
Arendt, Hannah 10, 13
Aristophanes 103
Aristotle: *Poetics* 80–83
Artaud, Antonin 4
Association of Presenters and Producers (APAP) conference 24
astonished actor 60
auteurs 2–6, 8, 11, 13–15, 23, 25–27, 30, 34, 40–43, 80; and actor 67; assumptions 77; impossibility 48–58; Japanese 68; lesbian 68; Viewpoints 70, 78; wrestles 85–86

Ball, William: *A Sense of Direction* 86
Barbagallo, Jess 5, 6, 7, 63, 64
Bartow, Arthur: *Training of the American Actor* 92
Bechtel, Alison: *Fun Home* 62
Behan, Brendan 53–57; *The Hostage* 55–56
Benning, Sadie 80
Berlant, Lauren 55
Berlin-Stinger, Laura 6, 7
Blackwell, Becca 5
Bogart, Anne 49, 68, 75, 78, 93
Brando, Marlon 76
Brecht, Bertolt 4, 49

Brook, Peter 4, 51
Brooks, David 5
Buckminster Fuller 53
Busch, Charles 29

Caine, Michael 49
Cameron, Jibz 33
captive audience 30, 34
Carnicke, Sharon Marie 92–93
Carra, Lawrence 84, 86–88; *Fundamentals of Play Directing* 86, 87
Chaikin, Joe: *The Presence of the Actor* 60
Chekhov, Michael 78, 107
Clurman, Harold: *On Directing* 86
color-blind casting 24–25
Coltrane, John 66–67
Connelly, Brendan 5
Courtney, Erin 80
Coward, Noël 88
Cunningham, Merce 27

Davey, Moyra 80
Dean, Alexander 84, 86–88; *Fundamentals of Play Directing* 86, 87
deep listening 38, 43–44, 88; American theater 39, 40; auteurs 41–43; *auteur theory* 40; bad acting 45–47, 46; coaches 41–43; given circumstances 38–39; play practice 41–45; practice 39; process 40–41; time-delays 43, 44; working process 40
Delaney, Shelagh 53–55; *A Taste of Honey* 53–54
Denis, Claire 3
Dickinson, Emily 38

directing 1–5, 23, 38–40, 49–53, 84; actors
    75–77; director education 74–79; play
    practice 44, 60, 68, 72; summer-stock play 42;
    teaching acting 81, 88; textbook 86–87, 103
Dolan, Jill 32
dominant (theater) culture 2
downtown theater 8, 30, 35
The Drama Review 29
dramaturgy 10, 26, 28, 51, 75, 95, 99, 100,
    107–108
Driscoll, Faye 33
Drum of the Waves of Horikawa 5, 6, *7–8*

Education of the Director 91, 93–94; acting
    coach 72, 77–79, 92; actors 75–77; casting
    77; diversification 79; doing directing
    74–80; gridwork 78–79; *Poetics* (Aristotle)
    80–82; publics 73; queer time 83; textbook
    84–88, 99, 103
Eichelberger, Ethyl 29
Emerson, Ralph Waldo 38
Essential Drama (Holdsworth) 53
Estevez, Emilio 62
The Estrangement Principle (Goldberg) 2
Euripides 103
experimental theater 29, 80
experimentation 14, 38

Fawaz, Ramzi 55
Fornes, Maria Irene 14
French New Wave 3
Fundamentals of Play Directing (Dean and
    Carra) 86, 87
Fun Home (Bechtel) 62

gay 33, 53, 55–56, 61
gaze 3
GAZR 24–25
Glaspell, Susan 72
Goldberg, Ariel: *The Estrangement Principle* 2
good actor 63–66
Grotowski, Jerzy 4, 5, 49, 75; *Towards a Poor
    Theater* 5

Hagen, Uta 78, 93
Harrison, Randy 33
Hobbes, Thomas: *Leviathan* 31
Hodge, Alison: *Actor Training* 92–93
Hodge, Francis: *Play Direction* 86
Holdsworth, Nadine 50, 53, 56; *Essential
    Drama* 53
The Hostage (Behan) 55–56
How a play is experienced (O'Harra) 10, *10*
How the audience receives information
    (O'Harra) 10, *11*
Hughes, Holly 29
Husiak, Laryssa 5, 6, 7

Ibsen, H. 107
I'm Bleeding All Over the Place project 1,
    17–22, 33, 37; audience 7–8, 10, 11, 14,
    15; auteur 2–6; Kabuki-mono 6; *A Living
    History Tour* 11, 12; Mischievium 5;
    performance event 3–4, 10; playwright
    13–14; politics and good theater 9–11;
    Publics and Counterpublics 8–9; queer 2,
    4–6; theater education 13

James, William 38
Japanese Theater 4
Jarcho, Julia 14
Jesurun, John 14, 29, 68, 69, 80–81
Jones, Elvin 67

Kabuki theater 4–6, 72, 79
Kaepernick, Colin 35
Kelly, John 29
Kennedy, Adrienne 13–14
Kron, Lisa 29, 62
Ksander, Peter 5

Laban, Rudolph 52
Lansbury, Angela 55
leadership 96
Lee, Young Jean 14
Lepides, Beth 29
lesbian 2, 6–9, 32, 38, 53, 60–63, 68, 72, 76
Leviathan (Hobbes) 31
Lincoln, Mary Todd 32
Littlewood, Joan *54*, 68, 72; American theater
    53; audience 48; auteur 55–57; Brecht
    theatre 58; Frogger 57–58; *Quare Fellow*
    53–55; rabbit hole 49–50; RADA 51;
    rehearsal process 48; Theater Workshop 52;
    West End 52, 56
A Living History Tour 4, 11
Love, Heather 55, 85

Maxwell, Richard 14
McBurney, Simon 48
McColl, Ewen 51
Meisner, Sanford 78
Meyerhold, Vsevolod 49, 50, 78, 93
Mikos, Mike 5, 96
Miranda, Daniela 83
Mnouchkine, Ariane 49, 75
Muñoz, José Esteban 9
Murrin, Tom 29

Noh theater 4, 41, 66, 72, 79

O'Harra, Brooke *10*, 10–12, *11*, *82*, *101*;
    How a play is experienced 10, *10*; *How the
    audience receives information* 10, *11*
Okada, Toshiki 97

Oliveros, Pauline 38, 43, 44
On Directing (Clurman) 86
O'Neal, Eugene 107
The Outsiders 62, *62*
Overlie, Mary 78

Parks, Suzan-Lori 13–14
performance events 3–4
Play Direction (Hodge) 86
playwrights 1, 3, 13–14, 28, 29, 48, 61–63, 66–68, 80, 81, 103, 106, 107
Poetics (Aristotle) 14, 80–82
Poetry Project 7
Pop Performance 29
The Presence of the Actor (Chaikin) 60
Price, Cedric 52
Proehl, Geoffrey 29
publics: audience 31–35; counterpublics 32–33; performance utopias 32–33; permission 30–31; queer 32–33; spectator 32

queer audience 8, 9
queer auteur 2–3
queerness 2, 6, 37, 83, 85

Raffles, Gerry 56
Rankin, Peter 50
"real people, not actors" 60–62
research-as-performance project 37
Robinson, Marilynne 37, 38, 80; *The Givenness of Things* 38
Room for Cream project 7–9, 32–33

Satter, Tina 14
Schreck, Heidi 5, 6, *6*, 63
Sedgwick, Eve Kosofsky 23, 53, 55; *Tendencies* 23
A Sense of Direction (Ball) 86
serial drama 7, 30, 69, 72
Shakespeare, W. 104, 107
Shaw, G.B. 88
Shawn, Wally 32
sightlines 25–26
Simon, Neil 88
Smith, Jack 29
Sophocles 103
spike marks 25
Sprang, James Allister 24

Stanislavsky, Konstanin 4, 39, 51, 78, 79, 88, 93; *An Actor Prepares* 51
Stanislavsky's system 4–5, 39, 49–51, 67, 78, 79, 88, 93
Stein, Gertrude 82, 83
Stevens, Wallace 38
Strasberg, Lee 78
Suzuki, Tadashi 49, 68, 93

A Taste of Honey (Delaney) 53–54
Tendencies (Sedgwick) 23
theater 1–3, 7–11, 15, 23–26, 49–56, 66–68, 73, 80, 107; audience 28, 30, 34; auteur 3, 4, 40, 80; commercial 62; contemporary moment 13; downtown 30, 35; dramaturgs 26; Dyke Division project 32; education 14, 42, 75, 81; experimental 29; Japanese 4, 5, 79; legacies 58; meta-theater 26; Mischievium 5; NYC 42; participatory 17, 33; person 14; physical space 26; playwrights 61; professional 42, 49; queer 29, 83; selection 4; space reclaim 27; Stanislavsky's system 78; structures 13; textbooks 103
The Givenness of Things (Robinson) 38
Towards a Poor Theater (Grotowski) 5
Townsend, Justin 5
Training of the American Actor (Bartow) 92
transgressions 34–35
Tropicana, Carmelita 29, 30

Vakhtangov, Yevgeny 50, 78
Valentine, Amber 33
Valk, Kate 80–81
Varda, Agnès 3
Viewpoints 68, 70, 78–79, 94

warm-ups 97–98
Warner, Michael 9, 30–31
Weems, Marianne 68
Weiss, Jeff 29, 30
Wellman, Mac 63
Wilson, Martha 33
Wilson, Robert 29

Zeami 43–44, 65–66, 93
Zorn, John 29

For Product Safety Concerns and Information please contact our EU
representative GPSR@taylorandfrancis.com
Taylor & Francis Verlag GmbH, Kaufingerstraße 24, 80331 München, Germany